PRAISE FOR *COLLATERAL DAMAGE*

"John Chirban wrote an amazing book for the resolution of family and children's issues. As a scientist and clinical psychologist, he deeply understands the steps for helping the children of divorce cope with the destruction of their worlds and family, and their need for the continuing assurance and love from their parents to be restored. It is clear that children are the real victims of family separation, but this does make them emotional cripples. With the steps noted in this valuable book, they can rebound with stronger bonds and meaningful skills to deal with both the beginning and ending of relationships."

—DR. FRANK LAWLIS
AUTHOR OF *NOT MY CHILD* AND *MENDING THE BROKEN BOND*

"We live in exponentially accelerating times of powerful technologies, solving many of humanity's grand challenges, yet the most basic needs of our children—safety, love, and family—are being destroyed by the pandemic of divorce. Dr. John Chirban's brilliant contribution of *Collateral Damage* presents a powerful antidote about how parents can change the negative consequences of divorce. Dr. Chirban's book unpacks the complications of divorce for children, providing clear and penetrating guidance for parents on a topic often too hard to confront, yet too detrimental to ignore."

—PETER H. DIAMANDIS, MD
FOUNDER AND EXECUTIVE CHAIRMAN, XPRIZE FOUNDATION
COFOUNDER AND EXECUTIVE CHAIRMAN, SINGULARITY UNIVERSITY
NEW YORK TIMES BESTSELLING AUTHOR, *ABUNDANCE* AND *BOLD*

"Dr. John Chirban's new book, *Collateral Damage,* is a must-read for parents who are in the process of separating or divorcing or who have divorced. It is both a professional and personal look at the effects of divorce on children and the pitfalls and possibilities for divorcing parents as they try to love, protect, and support their children and the family system that is dramatically changing. The most powerful contribution of Dr. Chirban's book is his ability to blend research findings and his own clinical and personal experience. Specific strategies are detailed for parents negotiating the challenges of helping children to emerge whole, confidant, and loved by their parents during the turmoil of transition. I strongly recommend this wonderful book and will refer other helping professionals and parents who want to learn more about how to avoid collateral damage to the children they care about."

—TOD GROSS, PSYD
DIRECTOR, ADAMS STREET ASSOCIATES

"Dr. Chirban is an accomplished scholar and clinician with a unique voice. In *Collateral Damage* he provides a road map for divorcing parents to protect and nurture their children while promoting their own emotional healing. His gentle wisdom is supported by data collected in his five-year study of thousands of divorcing parents and children of divorce, and through his own personal story. As a divorce lawyer of many years, I've learned that it is only by listening to the voices of children that we can discover and serve their real 'best interests.' I found *Collateral Damage* to be a practical resource that will be of immense guidance to families as they navigate their children through all stages of the divorce process."

—DONALD G. TYE
ATTORNEY AT LAW, PRINCE LOBEL TYE, LLP, BOSTON

"*Collateral Damage* is a *must*-read for all divorcing parents and for divorce professionals. With the Divorce Study, Dr. Chirban provides tangible evidence of the effects of divorce seen through the eyes of children. We are humbled by their voices and descriptions of their experiences. Only parents can mitigate the negative effects through honest listening and by working together to provide love and understanding and reduce conflict during and after the process of reconfiguring their family."

—ELIZABETH S. THAYER, PHD
COAUTHOR, *THE COPARENTING SURVIVAL GUIDE*

"Dr. Chirban's book reminds professionals and parents alike that there can be emotional casualties of divorce despite research indicating most children of divorce adapt well. His practical suggestions, based on his clinical experience, his research, and his personal history, will be helpful to parents considering divorce and to those already going through it. His advice to parents to utilize religious or spiritual resources is not often found in other writings on the subject and can be very useful to those so inclined."

—ROBERT ZIBBELL, PHD
FAMILY FORENSIC PSYCHOLOGIST AND PARENTING COORDINATOR
COAUTHOR, *EVALUATION FOR CHILD CUSTODY*

"In all of my years working as a psychiatrist, divorce is the trauma most often cited by my clients as life-changing. Though extremely painful for children and adults alike, there has been and always will be the hope of redemption and happiness on the other side. Thankfully, Dr. Chirban has made that hope a reality for thousands of families by providing a clear, concise, and practical guide for navigating this tumultuous transition. If you need help restoring wholeness to your family, Dr. Chirban's book is a must-read!"

—DAVID L. HENDERSON, MD
FOUNDER AND PRESIDENT, FOUR STONES COLLABORATIVE GROUP
AUTHOR, *MY TEENAGE ZOMBIE*

"Dr. Chirban's *Collateral Damage* urges parents to put their children's needs first—on all levels. Words alone are not enough. Thoughtful parents can, with the help of this book, understand not only how critical it is that they commit to managing their emotions and to a healthy, engaged style of parenting, but also have Dr. Chirban's practical wisdom and advice to aid them in this journey. For people of faith, he also gently reminds them that they can enrich and redirect their divorce inspired by their own and their children's spiritual life."

—ISOLINA RICCI, PHD
AUTHOR, *MOM'S HOUSE, DAD'S HOUSE*

"In *Collateral Damage*, Dr. Chirban has outlined an easy-to-read map of the emotional geography of divorce. Describing the parallel processes of parents and children, he provides definite suggestions and guidelines along with a clear rationale for each. Written in a language that makes this a guide for both psychologically-minded parents and those who are not, *Collateral Damage* is a handbook in which parents can easily access practical, age-appropriate help."

—CATHERINE McCALL
MARRIAGE AND FAMILY THERAPIST
CONTRIBUTING WRITER, *PSYCHOLOGY TODAY MAGAZINE*
UK BESTSELLING AUTHOR, *NEVER TELL*

COLLATERAL DAMAGE

Guiding and Protecting Your Child
Through the Minefield of Divorce

DR. JOHN T. CHIRBAN

W PUBLISHING GROUP

AN IMPRINT OF THOMAS NELSON

Published in Nashville, Tennessee, by W Publishing, an imprint of Thomas Nelson.

Thomas Nelson titles may be purchased in bulk for educational, business, fund-raising, or sales promotional use. For information, please e-mail SpecialMarkets@ThomasNelson.com.

Scripture quotations are taken from the New King James Version®. © 1982 by Thomas Nelson. Used by permission. All rights reserved.

Any Internet addresses, phone numbers, or company or product information printed in this book are offered as a resource and are not intended in any way to be or to imply an endorsement by Thomas Nelson, nor does Thomas Nelson vouch for the existence, content, or services of these sites, phone numbers, companies, or products beyond the life of this book.

ISBN 978-0-7180-8168-3 (eBook)

ISBN 978-0-7180-7988-8 (HC)

Library of Congress Cataloging-in-Publication Data

Library of Congress Control Number: 2016952236

Printed in the United States of America

17 18 19 20 21 LSC 10 9 8 7 6 5 4 3 2 1

To my youngest daughter
ARIANA MARIA

CONTENTS

FOREWORD

John Chirban is a master psychologist and theologian and an extremely intelligent author. With this book, he struck a major chord in my heart by raising awareness of the potential lifelong damage that plagues children of divorce. Kids have a personal truth—they believe what they believe about themselves—and that personal truth can be damaged when they live through a contentious divorce. This book is a lifesaving guide for parents who are divorced, are going through a separation, or are even just considering splitting up.

In the past fifteen years of the *Dr. Phil* show, I doubt that there has been a week go by that I have not seen at least one family in conflict and on the edge of—or having just gone through—divorce proceedings. I have seen the alienation efforts and the attempts to use the children as weapons against the other parent. More often than not, the children's emotions are totally neglected while the adults fight over meaningless issues.

This is not to demonize parents. In my observations, mothers and fathers do not intend to harm or neglect their children. I suspect that there is rarely a parent who does not love their kids; however, anger and frustration can overwhelm the circumstances and their emotions such that parents get defensive and lack focus. More often than not, parents don't have the guidance and abilities to cope with the tremendous stresses of their children's struggles in the divorce on top of their own.

John's book is more than a set of instructions for parents and children to ensure the maximum benefit from divorce. It fills the enormous gap created in these last generations in which divorce and separated families have become the mode of life. Health care professionals have made great effort in the literature about how to create meaningful and loving relationships, but little on how to end them, especially when children are involved.

My sincere desire would be for this book to become a guide and touchstone that helps divorcing or divorced parents realize they are models for their kids, and however they act or react will be observed and followed by their children. There are usually reasons for the termination of a relationship, but there must have been some good reason for its existence in the beginning. So if they do end, we must demonstrate how to do that with love and spiritual commitment. When parents commit to working together and set an example of healthy communication and active engagement, their children will emerge stronger and more resilient.

—DR. PHIL MCGRAW

ACKNOWLEDGMENTS

M y life has been blessed by many incredible experiences for which I am truly thankful—from opportunities to study with spiritual giants and Nobel Laureates at some of the finest institutions in the world, to working with some of the most talented leaders across disciplines for almost half a century. I am equally grateful to those from all walks of life who have opened up their lives to me and shared their stories during sessions of counseling and instruction in prisons, churches, schools, and hospitals. But like most parents, I have received no greater education, no greater miracle, no more powerful blessing than the gift of fatherhood for my children.

Like you, I always sought to impart my children with my absolute best and to enable them to reach their fullest potential. I feel graced as they have soared. Yet one severe blemish and unexpected turn in their journey from which I was unable to protect them has been the agony of my divorce. Like most parents, I would have never anticipated or chosen to subject them to this turn of events. We don't get to choose our destinies or challenges in life. Divorce unfolded as part of my journey. In the face of all the joys, particularly those shared with them, nothing could have befallen us that seemed more paradoxical, more clashing, and more dissident in their lives than divorce. It brought their jubilant lives to a screeching halt and could have turned them inside out, like a fatal crash. My instinct was to put their interests first, which allowed them to both survive and thrive. This book is a testimony to each of them: Ariana Maria, Anthony Thomas, and Alexis Georgia, each of whom has emerged as an inspiration in his or her own right throughout this process, and of whom I am most proud. They have evolved beautifully into adulthood to claim their own powerful passions and visions—a parent's dream.

This book is dedicated to Ariana Maria, my youngest daughter. It is *my honor* to honor her for her amazing determination to do her best in all areas of her life, to commit herself to her faith and God, and to lock her eye on her goals, remain balanced, and discern distractions. Ariana is blessed with purpose and gifts yet to be fully revealed. Though she is my youngest, she has always responded with astonishing maturity. Having graduated from high school with highest honors at sixteen as captain of varsity cheerleading, she is perceptive, persevering, competitive, and gracious. She retains her impressive academic and athletic standards as she begins her pre-med curriculum at the University of California, San Diego.

This dedication could never distract from the significance of Anthony and Alexis. Anthony studies physics and philosophy at Santa Clara University and explores the nature of "being." Alexis, the eldest, is pursuing a doctorate in clinical and sports psychology and is a competitive figure skater.

I have been honored to be represented by Jan Miller, my dear and respected friend and internationally recognized and gifted agent, who placed this book in the thoughtful, sensitive, and skilled hands of my editors, Debbie Wickwire and Meaghan Porter, at HarperCollins.

A research study and book is no small undertaking. This book's impressive results emerged through the conscientious efforts of the excellent staff that surrounded me. Two emerging scholars have especially helped me pull this book together, keeping me on my course through their dedication, energetic support, and attention to detail as exceptional researchers and editors: Julia Nash and Jesse J. Logan. I have felt exhilarated by their fresh insights and am continually grateful for their extraordinary personalities and tireless contributions. I also cannot adequately express appreciation for my dear friends and respected colleagues Dr. Yula Ponticas and Nicholas Graff, who have read this manuscript and offered their heartfelt and careful reviews in helping me shape early drafts of this book.

The tedious task of tabulating and converting qualitative data into quantitative data of more than ten thousand surveys was completed through the focused research skills of Rohit Goyal. Others faithfully assisting in the project, to whom I also express sincere appreciation, include my teaching and research assistants Peter Kavanaugh and Tyler Curry.

Finally, I am indebted to my valued friend and respected colleague Dr. Phil McGraw. His support and genuine interest in the development of this study permitted me to reach thousands of parents and children of divorce who participated in this study. Phil has been deeply supportive of the goals of this project and is genuinely committed to helping parents and children of divorce through his unprecedented contributions in media psychology where he has served an international audience.

BEFORE YOU BEGIN

Your Child and Your Divorce

I am a psychologist at Harvard Medical School and have taught classes
on family dynamics for more than thirty years. Throughout this time,
I have maintained a practice in psychotherapy to help both children and
adults deal with the emotional consequences of divorce.

While I have been well aware of the agony and disruption the breakup
of a family causes in the lives of children, my awareness deepened during
my own divorce. This wrenching process gave me firsthand experience
of the emotional impact that the dissolution of a marriage can have on
all members of a family. I realized that most parents—myself included—
have a great deal to learn and accept concerning the difficulties children
face during a divorce. Above all, I recognized that in order to successfully handle this challenge and its consequences, kids need most to feel
loved, protected, and supported.

After fifteen years of marriage, my wife and I were in the turmoil
of our divorce when our eleven-year-old son—the middle child of our
three—came to me in my home office one afternoon to bring me my
mail. Seeing him in the doorway was a welcome relief from the heavy
emotions I had been dealing with after yet another round of court filings,
which seemed to dominate my existence.

Before my son walked in, I'd been in a fog, exhausted and overwhelmed by the relentless stress divorce was placing on our home. The uncharacteristic disorder of my desk reflected the discord in my emotional life. I was working around the clock to maintain a sense of peace and normalcy for our three young children, yet the relative calm felt precarious and fragile. We seemed to be holding on to order with a white-knuckle grip.

Anthony entered my office with a smile, which appeared like a gift. He placed the mail on my desk, and we chatted about his day at school and the position he would be playing in his upcoming hockey game. After a few moments, he said, "I should probably get started on my homework."

When he left, it seemed as though there were less air in the room. I glanced at the pile of mail, and, with a sinking heart, I noticed a thick envelope. Another heavy legal filing of torment. Try as I might to keep them in check, my emotions got the best of me. I stood, reared back, and punched the wall in fury and frustration. Because I'm an academic and not a street brawler, I was initially impressed that my fist actually made a dent; then my despair returned. I braced myself against the wall and put one hand over my face, trying to hold back tears.

Suddenly, I felt small arms encircle my waist. I looked down and found that Anthony had returned upon hearing my outburst. He was doing his best to comfort me, the man who should be *his* source of comfort and security.

"Anthony, I am so sorry," I said. "This has just stirred up so much inside of me that . . ."

"I know, Dad," he said, not needing me to finish. "I know it's really hard on you right now."

His words tore at my heart. I had always seen myself as a firm and loving father—an authority figure who led by example, someone guided by values and faith. I sought to project strength, stability, and certainty to our children. Yet here I was, so torn apart that our eleven-year-old was compelled to offer me comfort and encouragement.

Our roles had reversed. The boy I'd so often reassured was now con-
soling me. It was a touching moment, but ultimately a wake-up call. This
moment marked a turning point in how I approached my torturous
divorce. I resolved to use all of my resources to find the best possible
way *to serve my kids*.

Before my divorce, I often counseled divorcing couples about how to
maintain self-control in front of their children. My counseling included
alerting parents to warning signs of when their children were suffering
and giving them ways to recognize and understand their disengagement in activity as a result of family turmoil. I offered detailed strategies
to help divorcing and divorced clients avoid conflicts and prevent disconnection from their kids. When Anthony put his arms around my
waist, it dawned on me that I hadn't followed my own advice. My son
reminded me that my primary focus must be on protecting my children
and providing them everything they needed to get through what would
become one of the most devastating events of their lives.

DIVORCE IN AMERICA

Everyone has heard the statistic that approximately 50 percent of marriages fail in the United States. However, this number doesn't include
the breakups by the increasing number of couples who never marry but
have children together. These breakups can be just as devastating to
children as a traditional divorce.

Even though divorce and family separations may be more socially
acceptable today, children still suffer greatly. While parents debate
who the victim is in the divorce, children are the ultimate victims.
If your children's sorrow and emotional issues are not addressed, the
cycle of divorce is likely to continue for them and for their children.
And, while they may appear resilient, children of divorce are more
likely to internalize their feelings and lose their bearings when proper
guidance is not provided. The statistics provided in this book reveal

that if children of divorced parents are not given what they need, they are more prone to drug and alcohol abuse, criminal behavior, mental and physical illness, and suicide, among several other negative consequences. We can better protect our children from the effects of fractured families.

Even the most thoughtful adults struggle with parenting challenges when dealing with the complications of divorce. Research documented in the coming pages confirms that divorce is devastating for children even when parents think they are monitoring their children's feelings closely. Children undoubtedly hurt more than they let on.

During the course of my divorce, when I asked my children how they were feeling, they would usually answer, "I'm fine." They'd answer the same way when I asked them how school had gone. Children rarely respond thoroughly to such questions about their feelings. I knew that I would learn more about what had actually occurred at school after spending quality time with them while taking a walk, throwing a football around, or chatting with them before they turned in for the night. My preoccupation with the legal battle of divorce and the demands of managing all of my children's needs was taxing. Yet I realized that these precious moments could not be sacrificed. I needed to learn what they were really thinking and how they were managing the changes in their lives. While I did not want my children to feel lost and unsupported during our divorce, I struggled to figure out what more I could do.

My own experience with the dissolution of my marriage inspired me to look deeper into this issue. So I began to research ways parents can stay focused on their children's needs by protecting and nurturing them, while also ensuring that they heal and continue to develop emotionally in the years that follow. I paid close attention to my children, and it made a difference. The progress they achieved academically, athletically, socially, and spiritually confirmed the significance of the path I chose. That research and my children's progress inspired this book.

THE DIVORCE STUDY

How do we as parents manage our own hurt, shock, anger, and despair so that we can give our children what they need? That question drove me to write this book; perhaps it is the one that has brought you here as well.

My experience with my son and daughters during my own divorce confronted me with far more questions than answers:

- What should my kids know about the divorce, and at what age?
- How can I tune in to them when I feel as though I'm drowning?
- How can I best protect their emotions during the loss of our family?
- How can I keep them on a solid foundation and a positive path to achieve their full potential?

The memory of my son putting his arms around my waist to console me stayed with me and drove me in my research. I wanted to achieve a deeper understanding of how parents can stay focused on their children during and after divorce so that fewer childhoods are damaged or lost when a marriage falls apart.

In addition to teaching, conducting research, and maintaining a psychotherapy practice, I serve on the advisory board for the *Dr. Phil* television show. Divorce and its impacts are discussed frequently on the show. Dr. Phil McGraw agreed with my belief that couples going through divorce are in need of parenting tools and guidelines to help their children, who often feel abandoned.

Phil supported my research and allowed me to use his show's enormously popular website to conduct a far-reaching divorce study that surveyed children and parents. The purpose of the surveys was to explore a much deeper understanding of what children go through in a divorce and what they need most from their parents during this difficult time.

Through the Divorce Study, we asked children about the impact of divorce on their lives and relationships. We also asked parents to tell us how they met their children's needs during and after the divorce. We received more than ten thousand responses from the Divorce Study surveys. The concerns from children define the targets of this book.

The results from the Divorce Study reveal one painful yet undeniable fact: whether a divorce is amicable or acrimonious, children often feel alone, unheard, and rejected. The most striking finding of the Divorce Study is the dramatic disparity between the ways parents and their children assess the impact of divorce. Most parents do not recognize how disruptive divorce is for their children and do not respond to their children's needs. From the most significant issues raised during the Divorce Study, I identified nine of the greatest parental oversights made during and after a divorce. In the following nine chapters, I address each of these issues and recommend positive resolutions for how you can step up and guide your children through this traumatic period.

Against the background of conflicting studies that suggest divorce does not transfer devastating effects to children (like social stigma, for instance), the Divorce Study confirms that for children, the consequences of divorce are not only real but also destructive.

In addition to answering quantitative questions, people who participated in the Divorce Study provided qualitative responses that elaborated on their situations. These responses, when analyzed and combined with my other research, showed that children of divorce experience more challenges than their peers who have not gone through the same trauma. They have poorer health, greater insecurities, and more problems in school and relationships. They also are more prone to have children out of wedlock, suffer from emotional problems, and exhibit difficulties with problem-solving. An alarming number of children who do not receive proper guidance from adults self-medicate with alcohol, drugs, and other high-risk behaviors to fill the absence of quality parenting. When parents are too overwhelmed to give their children what they need, children are vulnerable and at greater risk for succumbing to the influence of peers in addition to potential predatory forces, such as street gangs, drug dealers, pimps, and pedophiles.

Children of divorce learn quickly not to say what they feel or ask for what they need. They may feign a game face because they don't want to be a greater burden on their parents or because they feel their parents can't really hear or understand their pain. Divorcing or divorced parents will find it especially helpful to their children and to their developing relationships if they understand and vigilantly respond to meet their children's needs. Unless these needs are met, their children are more likely to become another statistic and one day experience divorce themselves—a phenomenon known as the *divorce cycle* or the *intergenerational transmission of divorce.*

My research leaves little doubt that unless parents address the challenges of divorce for their children, it will be a harmful turning point in their lives. The Divorce Study and other national studies reveal huge disconnects between the perceptions of parents and children during a divorce and its aftermath. These facts are hard to hear! The findings from the Divorce Study illustrate where that disconnect begins:

- While 51 percent of parents felt that they were responsive to their children during their divorce, 72 percent of children said their parents did not do a good job managing the divorce for them.
- More than half of children (52 percent) felt they were drawn into their parents' battle, even in those divorces that were not described as "contentious" or "acrimonious."

My ex-spouse sued me for full custody and modified child support—with no ability or intention of taking the children as a full-time responsibility. The children began to live out of a suitcase every other week, and they had sleeping problems due to the new environment and the threat of losing the home they had always had with me, not to mention the anticipation for having to face a judge at trial.

—*Parent (married twelve years)**

* Respondents identified as "Parent" are divorced parents. The time frame in parentheses refers to the length of the parents' marriage before divorce.

The Divorce Study also helped explain why so many children feel lost both during and after divorce:

- Eighty percent of children said that they did not express themselves about the divorce.
- Eight-four percent of parents recognized that their divorce had a negative impact on their child's life—with 80 percent reporting a long-term effect on their children.

I went from being top of my class to just barely scraping through. I feel like I was robbed of a stable, happy home. I feel like I was robbed of an opportunity to gain a good education. I was robbed of the security, stability, and support that I needed at a crucial time in my development to help me become a well-balanced, emotionally strong woman who felt secure with who she was and of her abilities and talents.

*—Forty-year-old (age eighteen at the time of divorce)***

But adequate parenting is not the only resource found lacking for children during divorce:

- Nearly seven out of ten children (67 percent) who underwent professional therapy during their parents' divorce said the therapy was "unhelpful" or "a waste of time."

This is another one of many resounding reasons why parents will find it important to remain focused on being the guiding influence in their children's lives during this challenging time. While it is responsible to seek additional support for our children when we are preoccupied by the demands of divorce, we need to assess whether these supportive efforts actually enhance our children's lives.

** Respondents identified by age are children of divorce. The time frame in parentheses refers to the respondent's age at the time of his or her parents' divorce.

Our children are our most precious gifts. We have a limited amount of time to help them build solid foundations. Most parents seek to be the best guides and role models they can—but divorce is a minefield, and children become collateral damage. We can do a better job of guiding our children through that minefield. I hope this book will serve as your wake-up call and as a resource to help you be the parent your children deserve, even when you are overwhelmed by and immersed in your divorce. Our children are our primary focus no matter what else is going on in our lives. That is our undeniable responsibility as parents.

How to Use This Book

This book explains how children become collateral damage during and after divorce and gives practical advice on how you can become a better guide for your children even when you are devastated and distracted. My research confirms how childhoods may be lost and, as a result, the children of divorce often enter adulthood prematurely (as "parentified" children), carrying serious emotional deficits. I will explain how you can better serve the your children's needs and avoid common parenting failures during this critical time.

This book includes true stories from both parents and children experiencing divorce and its aftermath. Names have been changed to protect the identities of those involved. The advice, self-reflective questions, and strategies provided throughout are based on comprehensive research from the Divorce Study, documented studies, and my extensive professional interactions in both divorce court and my private therapeutic practice. You have already read a couple of excerpts from the Divorce Study in which respondents demonstrate the concerns this book addresses. Such personal reflections and insights are highlighted throughout the text.

Part 1 addresses the plight of children during their parents' divorce; part 2 addresses the parents' struggles in view of their children. This book focuses on facts especially related to your children. It is not written to frighten you about things that could go wrong, browbeating you or telling you what you need to do during this rough time. This is a book full of solutions in view of realities children face. It does not accentuate guilt; rather, it includes suggestions for healing and caring for yourself so that you retain your invaluable role as a viable parent and maintain your family. Some of what you read will be hard, but it is rewarding and worth your time. Each chapter opens with a call to action or "Parental Oversight" that I recommend addressing with your child, and ends with "Parental Recommendations" or practical suggestions for moving forward. Within these pages, you'll find applicable information and the tools to help you support your children at a time when they need you most.

By the end of this book, you will understand what your children's needs are and how to effectively negotiate them in your role as a parent of children of divorce. I will help you find ways to communicate with your kids so they feel comfortable confiding in you at a time when their foundation of trust has been damaged, and I will guide you toward ways to keep those critical lines of communication open. I will help you open windows into your children's minds and emotions and show you how to be with them most effectively.

Do you feel that you understand your children's needs? Do you think they can share their struggles with you? Are you preparing them to be adults capable of having lasting and loving relationships despite your own divorce? Do you have the answers they need when they ask about your divorce? While these matters can be painful to read about and the questions too difficult to answer, it is crucial that these answers are in your hands. If you can honestly answer no to any of these questions, or if you are uncertain about how to respond, then this book is especially for you.

By picking up this book, you've taken a courageous and critical step toward protecting the well-being and future of your children. The fact that you've chosen to read this book shows your commitment to help your children feel that they are loved, protected, and supported during and after your divorce. The journey will be challenging, but we can do this. Let's dig in together to learn how to better understand our children's needs so that we can successfully maintain our role as solid and effective parents.

Part 1

GUIDING AND PROTECTING YOUR CHILDREN

Chapter 1

ATTUNE TO YOUR CHILD

I came to understand that a parent's pain is alleviated when they choose to divorce and get away from each other. But I also discovered that their pain is inadvertently placed onto their child and the child becomes the recipient of two people's pain. No matter how much counseling the child receives or how well the parents handle the process, their pain is transferred to their child. It is ultimately the child that has to pay for the parents' divorce.

—PARENT (MARRIED EIGHTEEN YEARS)

Parental Oversight 1

During the throes of divorce, you may tune out your children, leaving them alone to manage the separation of the family. When you are un-aware of your children's needs, you may not engage in effective com-munication with them, missing an invaluable and critical opportunity to bond as they try to sort through their thoughts and feelings about the shake-up of divorce.

> I felt horrible. No one told me. I just knew because of the fights. When my father eventually left, I knew that he would never come back to me. I felt worthless and lonely, primarily because my

mother had some issues and should not have been left alone with me and my two sisters. I felt neglected by my father.

—Twenty-six-year-old (age six at the time of divorce)

It was very awkward. They brought us into the kitchen, sat us down, and they said they were separating. Who did we want to live with? We were fourteen and twelve. It was like, "Huh? What do you mean who do we want to live with?" Ridiculous.

—Fifty-one-year-old (age fourteen at the time of divorce)

[I was] totally devastated. They were always affectionate, and repeatedly assured my sister and I that we would never have to worry about them divorcing. Then they did! I felt so insecure and unsafe. I thought I had caused the divorce because I didn't make good grades and my sister and I argued sometimes. I felt abandoned because both my parents were more concerned with their personal grief than me or my sister.

—Thirty-six-year-old (age eleven at the time of divorce)

Let's try to understand what's going on inside the hearts and minds of our children by hearing how a young woman struggled with her parents' divorce throughout her life, though she was only an infant when her parents divorced.

MAYA'S STORY (PART 1)

My parents had no idea how much their divorce affected me. I struggled with my ability to share my feelings and thoughts about what it means to have a healthy and open dialogue and relationship with them until I told them a couple years ago how I was feeling. I was in my early twenties.

To be fair, I struggled to understand the dynamic between my mother and father—how difficult the decision must have been to divorce and how it affected their own emotional well-being. I was only a baby when the divorce took place; and as I grew older, I became more aware.

I was used to dividing my weekends between my primary household, which was my mom's place, and spending time with my dad at his duplex, along with my grandparents. In hindsight, I was able to spend a significant amount of time with my grandparents, who were consistently there for my brother and me, especially when my father was not. In addition, my parents were never on good terms. Often my brother and I witnessed our parents bickering about each other in front of us; to say it was heart-wrenching is an understatement. It became worse when my father was diagnosed with severe depression.

When I attempted to talk about the divorce and my feelings, my mother shut down and all order in my life turned to chaos. Her responses echoed bitterness, resentment, and remorse as she always finished each brief exchange of dialogue with, "I'm sorry. I wish you had a better father." All of this is to say, the consequences of divorce continued well after it was finalized. Addressing these areas of concern is critical. There is strength in letting one's guard down to have a genuine conversation between parent and child concerning what's next, and in being present, not caught up in the mental cloud of divorce chaos.

—*Twenty-five-year-old (age six months at the time of divorce)*

We may be surprised by the insidious damage of divorce when it occurs before a child has learned to walk, or when we perceive our divorce as amicable. In the face of the family's breakdown, were Maya's parents effectively attuned to her needs? What do you think might have calmed her anguish? Did they approach the divorce in her "best interest"?

As you read this chapter, think about why children are so deeply affected by their parents' divorce. What can you do to meet your children's needs and avoid permanent scarring? Let's begin by taking a closer look at the potentially damaging side effects children of divorce face.

Children's Needs and the Impact of Divorce

Human beings are wired for attachment and the experience of love.[1] We instinctively smile at newborns because they are magnets of affection—our smiles are a response to both their needs and our innate design for human contact. When children are isolated or deprived of their instinctive desire to connect, to relate, and to love, they implode. This implosion leads to a longing for what is not provided in the home: love and nurturance. In response to deprivation of needed contact, children often act out in isolation and search for love elsewhere. They require substantive, attentive nurturing to thrive. The supportive love of parents fuels the achievement of children's potential. By recognizing the need to relate effectively to others, to love and be loved, we impart the capacity for healthy intimacy and generosity in infants, setting the tone for how they continue to develop.

Through our actions, we further impart the ability to confront expected and unexpected challenges with resilience and understanding. Divorce can rob children of their natural developmental process and their ability to access the confidence they were given from the most important people in their lives: their parents. Their role models may be removed or preoccupied. This, we know, has lasting effects. Children who experience early traumatic stress, such as separation from a primary caregiver, are prone to long-term effects of mental and cognitive dysfunction in adulthood.[2]

Your child's ability to overcome the potential negative impact of your divorce may be pre-wired from birth—based on the strengths and weaknesses of his or her genetic makeup and personality, as well as his or her provided support system.[3] Nonetheless, child psychologists have convincingly explained that kids require attentive nurturing through-out their growth if they are to master unique challenges at each stage of their development, including adulthood. As the Divorce Study confirms, when parents divorce—even during their child's adulthood—loss of familial security causes deep emotional wounds.

Research reveals disturbing information about the plight for children of divorce: when the family structure breaks, the children turn elsewhere, often to peers and the media, and may embrace deviancy and recklessness.[4] They may act out for needed attention and become primary targets for street gangs, drug dealers, and sexual abuse.[5] Children of divorce are more likely to be involved in crime and die at younger ages than children from intact homes, and they are also more prone to suicide.[6] When they get older, children of divorce are more likely to go through a divorce themselves and to bear children out of wedlock. Adults with divorced parents are 38 percent more likely to have a divorce themselves than adults raised in intact families.[7]

> In college, I had several friends whose parents divorced once they were out of the house. It was equally as hurtful. [My friends] started drinking and sleeping around. It was painful to watch. As their friend, I watched it; and their parents conveniently lived on in delusion that because the kid was eighteen and at college that this would somehow magically not hurt them. [They were] insensitive and selfish.
>
> —Thirty-nine-year-old (age fourteen at the time of divorce)

Although the struggles of children of divorce have been well documented, **the combined research from independent studies on divorce report conflicting outcomes for children—and cite both positive and negative results.** Some studies claim that because divorce is so commonplace in our society, it is not possible to isolate it as the sole cause of poor behavior in children of divorce.[8] Other studies highlight that there are advantages and even secondary gains for children of divorce, such as developing stronger resilience and having options for living situations that they would not otherwise have had.[9]

Such encouraging findings were not confirmed by the results of the Divorce Study and appear counterintuitive given the distress children reported concerning their experiences. While it is important to recognize that positive aspects of divorce may occur when a child or parent is exposed to violence and abuse, **the predominant trend reported in the Divorce Study makes clear that adversity resulting from the divorce is widespread and prevalent. The surveys from the Divorce Study also offer insight into how to respond to hurtful aspects of this agonizing event.** (This subject is addressed in chapters 5 and 6.)

In my clinical practice, I've observed—and a broad range of research supports—that children of divorce experience many more negative consequences in life than children from intact families. As stated in the introduction, the deficits that children of divorce experience include

- poorer health
- emotional problems
- trouble with problem-solving
- lower academic performance
- increased danger of dropping out of school
- difficulties maintaining relationships and retaining future employment[10]

Despite the growing norm of single-parent homes, the cycle continues to drain the psychological well-being of children and perpetuates their lower academic achievement and the potential for difficult life outcomes.[11] I'd be remiss not to report that female children of divorce generally experience more negative long-term repercussions than those of non-divorced families.[12]

The Divorce Study revealed that 76 percent of children stated that the divorce "affected their life negatively." **It doesn't have to be that way for your children.** If you picked up this book, you probably want to know what occurs for children during divorce and what you can do to help your kids avoid these negative consequences. Despite the fact that studies generally confirm statistics regarding devastating scenarios, **children of divorce are *not* condemned to a future life of failure, deviance, or death. The good news is that the impact of divorce for your children is within *your* control.**

How you approach your children during your divorce is what most significantly affects the future of their lives. How you love them, nurture them, and secure the structure of the home, while maintaining authority[13] before, during, and after divorce, greatly affects the success of your child's adaptation following the divorce.[14]

The quality of *your* parenting is the single most important factor for saving your child from becoming a statistic of collateral damage stemming from divorce. Rather than looking at the impact of divorce as inevitable and fixed, look at the root of this problem and recognize the negative feelings and thoughts your children may be wrestling with. Left unaddressed, these forces can build up over the course of their lifetimes. Your children's sense of loss of love greatly factors into their stability.

Now consider Maya, whose story opened this chapter. Her parents divorced when she was six months old. Do you see how her home life affected her emotionally? Were her parents attuned to the impact that their divorce had on her? Can you identify ways they responded that intensified her distress? What may have occurred to minimize her despair?

YOUR ACTION MESSAGE TO YOUR CHILD

In another publication, I described how parents can effectively communicate messages of genuine love to their children:[15]

- *I see you. You are important and invaluable, and you know it.*
- *I love you and act in ways that show it.*

- *I recognize you and take time to give you the attention you deserve, and we celebrate it.*
- *I guide you to discover your True Self that shapes your identity, dignity, and direction and embrace it.*

Through the messages of your active love, *you*, as a parent, impart the tools your children need so they develop soundly.

In the midst of divorce, communicating this is no small order. Both you and your partner are disengaged from each other—you are no longer in sync, and you can no longer depend on each other. You both carry the weight of numerous stressors in multiple areas of your lives. You are not in optimal control. You do not have the benefit of time and patience. Plus, you are frequently fatigued during the roller coaster of the divorce process. You feel depleted.

> My daughter was two and a half years old when we divorced; and now she's twenty-seven. As she grew up, she always had anxieties and fears that men would never stay—that they would always leave her. When she had a boyfriend at age sixteen, she felt she "needed" that guy and was terrified he'd leave. When they broke up, she was a basket case. . . . It took me years of talking to her, reinforcing her mind with the thoughts that she needs to be happy with herself—and never dependent on any man—until she learned to be strong and independent. . . . She is now twenty-seven. And I can say that through patience and support from myself (her mom), she is a strong, happy, self-supporting, positive person who now "wants" a man but does not "need" a man. I'm so proud of her.
>
> —*Parent (married nine years)*

It is best for children if both parents act collaboratively and constructively in managing their divorce, yet this is not always possible. Even when divorce is not contentious, it makes great demands on both parties.

Nonetheless, **if only one parent recognizes and responds to his or her children's needs through active parenting, that parent can secure a solid pathway for the development of healthy children.** In the following pages, you will read several accounts of children who suffered considerably because of the actions and unintended injuries their parents caused during divorce. By attuning yourself to your children's needs, you can rescue them from the overbearing weight of carrying this adult situation.

> Eighteen years of a dysfunctional marriage is a long time. I also felt validated to be told what I always knew: that there was no love between them for one another. But I never said this. It seems that now as an adult, I am affected by their past actions. Now I have feelings and questions that lay on my heart. As a result, I have troubles with my boyfriend, and our own common-law relationship is suffering.
>
> —*Twenty-eight-year-old (age seventeen at the time of divorce)*

> I think the fact that they avoided speaking ill of one another, for the most part, was extremely helpful. Whatever grudges they might have had, they never subjected us to them. It made it easier to see them as people. Neither of them ever played a victim role either, so it made it easier for us to live our lives as adults who had to be responsible for the good and bad that we had garnered.
>
> —*Forty-three-year-old (age three at the time of divorce)*

Though unpleasant, divorce is sometimes a wise choice when it improves circumstances, such as parental struggles, and protects family members—especially from abusive situations. It is important to recognize that although some parents may not formally divorce, they may essentially be living as if divorced because their marriages lack love and exhibit discord. Children within these intact but practically split homes often suffer some of the same problematic repercussions of children of divorce. The interpersonal dynamics between these family members express signs of divorced parents, such as fighting, negativity, and distress—all of which generate similar destructive consequences. While parents may act relatively casual about the distress, their children may be imploding because no one has recognized the impact the discord imposes on them.

> When I graduated from college, my father gave me a diamond ring as a present. When my mother saw the ring, she informed me that this ring was her engagement ring that he had claimed had been stolen during the divorce. She wanted the ring back. Here I was, twenty-two, and still right in the middle of their games.
>
> —*Forty-eight-year-old (age ten at the time of divorce)*

Parental discord breaks apart the marriage, the family, and the home. For children, divorce is the dissolution of the family's foundation. Though divorce may be an appropriate "breaking apart" of a dysfunctional marriage, we need to manage this process to protect our children from the minefield of divorce. Otherwise, it can lead to the "breaking apart" of our children. Divorce can fracture children's capacity for identity formation, which may have lasting consequences. In Maya's case, even though she was only an infant when her parents divorced, the reverberations from the event still actively damaged her years later.

"In the Best Interest of the Children"

All parties in the divorce process—the plaintiff, the defendant, and the court—argue that their primary consideration is what's "in the best interest of the children." This phrase implies a commitment to being tuned in to children's physical, emotional, developmental, and spiritual needs. Yet children are often forgotten during the divorce process. Even courts describe their primary concern as serving "the best interest of the children"—yet kids are usually absent from any legal proceedings, though several states permit a potential role for their voice in the process.

Some judges I work with claim that their primary concern is serving the best interest of the children, but they still refuse to interact with the children of divorce before rendering their decision of custody. Some claim that they do not want to cause further distress to the children by bringing them into court. Others admit that they are not trained to work with children and do not know what to say to them, especially regarding the high-stakes situation they're in.

Should children remain outside of divorce proceedings? The answer is both yes and no. Children should not be drawn into the adult particulars of the marital struggle. Studies have long confirmed that parents who argue in front of their children cause the greatest emotional damage.[16] However, if we are truly committed to acting in our children's best interest and staying tuned in to what they need, then we must allow them a voice when they have already been dragged into a bitter conflict.

> I felt like I didn't have any support to help me adequately explain the divorce and all it entailed. I definitely couldn't afford to pay for help. I just felt very alone and in the dark. Since I felt like that, I am sure my kids felt even more lost.
>
> —Parent (married one year)

My clinical experience, particularly in highly contentious divorces, confirms that children embroiled in legal issues and seriously affected by court actions are much more distressed by being shut out of the proceedings related to their welfare than they would be if they had an opportunity to meet with a judge. In such situations, it appears that the judge could render more informed decisions if he or she heard from the children. For kids who have been exposed to abuse or have witnessed dangerous behavior from their parents, the risk of the courts further victimizing them by prohibiting or discounting their voices is greater than the harm that comes from a stressful legal process.

If they feel it is pertinent, some judges in some states meet with the children before rendering custody decisions; however, such accommodations are often unavailable to children, and, as you have already read from children in the Divorce Study, their own parents often distance them from information about the divorce process. It's essential for your children to learn about your divorce from you in a manner that best protects parent-child boundaries and your children's needs.

For now, as a starting point, let's consider the extent to which you're already dialed in to what your children need. The answers to these questions may help you see places where you've inadvertently tuned out:

- Do they know about the divorce? If so, how did they respond?
- What do they understand about the impact of divorce for the family?
- Are you at ease with how they are managing news of the divorce?
- Do you think they are at ease with managing news of the divorce?
- Do you feel they can speak with you about their feelings and concerns? Have you asked them to share their feelings with you— and do you make yourself available?
- How do you plan to support "the best interest" of your children during your divorce?

TELLING YOUR CHILDREN ABOUT DIVORCE

While you may have been anticipating divorce for some time, your children are often caught unaware. Talking about divorce requires sensitivity to its many aspects, particularly as it affects your relationship with your children. By the time your kids learn that you're headed for divorce, there is little anyone can do to stop the train from barreling down the tracks. How has news about the divorce affected your children? Have you embraced their unique process?

One of the most difficult conversations you will have with your children is the one where you tell them that you and your spouse are getting divorced. Through the responses to the Divorce Study, I have observed the myriad ways in which parents manage this difficult discussion. Sometimes, children find out that the family is breaking up when one of the parents moves out of the house, seemingly without explanation. Other times, kids are given the bad news with no one to console them. And sometimes, parents get it and systematically work with their children to ease the substantial adjustment.

> My dad walked in on a Sunday morning and said to all of us, "I have something to tell you. It might make you happy, it might make you sad; but I am not happy, and I am leaving." My brother, mom, and I were all sitting there like, "What just happened?" I know that my dad abandoned us after having an affair with a woman whom he married after my parents divorced.
>
> —*Thirty-five-year-old (age twelve at the time of divorce)*

Parents need to provide information and communicate in a manner that is age appropriate. Addressing your five-year-old and your fifteen-year-old about the impending divorce are two very different conversations. With your five-year-old, you may introduce the subject by saying, "Mommy and Daddy always love you and will always be with you to keep you safe, but we are going to be living in two different homes." In the case of your fifteen-year-old, who is acutely aware of romantic relationships and the impact of divorce, a more detailed exchange is necessary. (Chapter 7 identifies the developmental needs and recommendations for this conversation.) While both children will have many concerns about this major environmental and relational change, the needs and concerns of the particular children are different, and giving either too much or too little information could create problems. So we need to be attuned to the individual souls.

In the Divorce Study, children characterized news of their parents' divorce in disturbing terms: "It ripped me apart." "I had nowhere to turn." "The most traumatic experience of my life." "Agonizing like nothing else I could imagine." "It brought me to consider ending my life." The Divorce Study revealed that 49 percent of parents reported not discussing their children's feelings about their divorce, while 57 percent of children stated that their parents did not do much at all. In this study, children shared that they were rarely asked how they felt and said they believed their parents' actions during the divorce did not have their best interests in mind.

Fear is among the most potent and disastrous emotions in human life. **Divorce is scary for parents, but it ushers in torrential forces of fear for children. The Divorce Study found that 73 percent of children expressed fears regarding the "family breaking up," with only 19 percent claiming "no fears," and 8 percent stating that "the choice between mother or father" was "most frightening."** In this way, divorce fractures a child's identity formation, which may have lasting consequences.

When the reality of divorce invaded my home, I felt the avalanche threatening to tear apart my children's foundation. My first impulse was to stop the event from occurring, but as I found it was beyond my control, I recognized that our children—who were all in elementary school—were like sheep being led to their slaughter. I saw them as the *only* innocent victims and recognized their need for attention and support, since they were dependent in most every way.

Ariana's Response

During my own divorce, tensions were at a fever pitch. The night our children got wind that we might divorce, they were in shock and emotionally distraught. Strikingly, our seven-year-old daughter used the computer to write a succinct yet poignant e-mail to my wife and me. It read:

Dear Mom and Dad,

　　It will *brake* my heart in two if you will *divorce*.

Love,

Ariana

Ariana's description vividly described her visceral pain. Her image clearly revealed her agony in concrete terms, with symbolic expression of her fear—the breaking of her heart. After reading the e-mail, I found her alone in her room. She was lying on her bed, staring blankly, as if devoid of feelings. I asked if we could talk about what she was thinking and feeling. She sat quietly. After some prompting, tears filled her eyes, and she said, "I'm worried about what will happen next."

I asked her what she imagined would happen. At that point, she climbed on my lap and hugged me, and with giant tears streaming down her face, she said, "I'm very sad." After a few moments, she added, "Does this mean that I will also divorce after I get married?"

Ariana's mind was churning not only about the imminent threat of the breakup of our home but also about the loss and devastation she would endure as a result of the divorce in her future.

I assured Ariana that her parents' divorce did not mean that she would also divorce—though I was struck that she so unknowingly raised the statistically significant possibility that she, too, may divorce one day.

In these moments, it is important to directly acknowledge your child's specific uncertainties. Your words confirm that you hear your child and that he or she is not alone. By responding the best you can to your children's concerns, you will fill their loneliness and uncertainty *with the security only a parent can provide*. In my home, we spent time discussing how disturbing divorce could be in terms that my young children could understand. By sharing their fears, fantasies, and nightmares, they released their pain and found that they were, in fact, not alone. I expressed that we can't always control what occurs in relationships. Best friends can move out of town. People can develop new interests that lead them away from us. Even parents can realize that their relationship is not working as they had hoped. I assured Ariana that she would not be alone—that she would always have her parents with her. However, only when we come through for our children do they know they can count on us. Only then can the uncertainty find resolution.

Loss of security and abandonment are what the majority of children fear most about divorce.[17] Each child experiences and expresses different feelings with different reactions. By tuning in to how each child is managing changes—actually and specifically answering this question for each of our children—we can begin to understand their experiences. The proverb "still waters run deep" is particularly apt here. You should not believe for one minute that a child who is placid about news of his or her parents' divorce has no concerns. That child should be watched most closely.

> It takes a while for the fear and frustration to really sink in, and when the life changes start happening (moving, two houses, etc.), as a kid, you really need help with how to manage your feelings and your parents. Plus, I think as a kid in the middle of a divorce, you shut down emotionally, and it can take time to get past the "Oh, no, I'm fine" barrier.
> —*Twenty-six-year-old (age nine at the time of divorce)*

> At the time, I was so pissed and had no idea what to do or say. We went to family counseling once, and I wore fishing lure earrings, had black streaks in my hair, smoked, and couldn't have given a shit about anything. I didn't want to talk at that point. I wanted to beat the shit out of something, but I had no release.
> —*Forty-year-old (age fourteen at the time of divorce)*

It occurred to me that Ariana's e-mail to us was a medium that allowed her to express her feelings and communicate with her mother and me. I had encouraged our children to write their thoughts, feelings, or drawings in a diary and e-mail me anytime—which she did. Inviting your children to express their feelings with you or to themselves helps them begin dealing with what is occurring in their lives, rather than running away from it and themselves.

At one point, Ariana started drumming on pots and pans with a spoon. It seemed clear that she was expressing intense feelings that she may not have had any words for. So I asked if she wanted a drum set for Christmas. She loved that idea. We got her not only a secondhand drum set she could let loose on but also a drum instructor who helped her play music from her favorite songs. However, I think just banging was her real interest.

When I discussed Ariana's progress with her second-grade teacher, her attunement to and anticipation of Ariana's nonverbal distress impressed me. She came up with the idea of a "ripping notebook." This private notebook was for drawing, writing, or releasing feelings or expressing anything that came to Ariana's head—or for her just to rip those painful feelings apart. I mention all this to encourage you to figure out activities that show your children that you know they are dealing with difficult feelings, and that you encourage activities that help them access and express their feelings. Show them you understand that dealing with the divorce may be very hard for them. By doing so, you are tuning in to their needs.

The Divorce Study confirmed that when parents don't know what to say and how to respond directly to their child, it paralyzes and halts them from communicating at all.

Many parents respond by announcing the divorce to the children and behaving as though the announcement alone is sufficient. In fact, telling your children about the divorce is merely an introduction, requiring much further explanation and discussion. According to the Divorce Study, only 3 percent of children found their parents to be "understanding and supportive" as they disclosed their plan to divorce. This reveals a very low percentage of children who received the compassion and love necessary for their well-being.

Remember, as hard as it is for parents, it is even more painful for children who do not know or understand what's going on. Children struggle to understand their fears and concerns. They want their parents united so they feel safe and free to be kids. They naturally seek a secure foundation. Announcement of a divorce triggers a seismic attack to their security, and the aftershock, or the manner in which you respond or don't respond after the news, can be even more cataclysmic.

Even in homes where kids are at the center of their parents' attention, divorce shoves children to the background as parents become preoccupied and stressed with their own worries and needs. Too often, parents perceive themselves as the only victims of divorce.

It's no wonder that parents act as if announcing the divorce is enough. Because of their own understandable and overwhelming distress, parents do not know what to say or how to say it. And, in the Divorce Study, **72 percent of parents confessed regret for the impact their divorce had on their children, and a majority of parents described feeling guilty for the part they played in the divorce.** Parents may defend against their guilt with denial and rationalization, failing to recognize or confront the increased torment and fear that develops when their children are placed in a position to absorb this unsettling news without a means by which to process it.

SETH'S STORY

I am reminded of twelve-year-old Seth, who confronted his mother upon learning of her plan to divorce his father. Distraught by this news, Seth gathered information from the Internet about what happens to kids of divorce. He chose to channel his anxiety in this constructive direction, and his research led him to conclude that parents usually don't divorce when children are in middle school. Consistent with the defenses of a boy his age, he did not break down in tears or sadness but used facts from the Internet to argue that his family should stay together. He presented his mother with his findings.

"Divorce is adult business, and this doesn't concern you!" Seth's mother responded in an effort to shut down the conversation. Engulfed by her own distress and inattentive to the emotional impact divorce would have on her son, she could not hear his plea. Seth continued to press her with statistics in an effort to appeal his parents' decision to divorce. But because he felt continually rebuffed by his mother, he eventually backed down. He internalized his distress, which turned to fury, and he detached from her. Seth's mother missed his invitation to talk about the details of why the divorce occurred, and she neglected to respond to what was underneath his Internet investigation: his hurt, worry, and pain.

Seth's mother's unavailability is both understandable and common during divorce. Emotions run high. But **slow down; be aware, alert, and open to your thoughts, feelings, and moods—and recognize their impact on your children—so you are clear minded and available to your children when they need you most.**

I cannot tell you how often patients who were children of divorce have told me that their parents said, "The divorce is none of your business," "This doesn't concern you," or "This is between your father and me." **Of course the divorce is the child's business! His or her family is at risk. The very structure and existence of the child's home is called into question.** Just as much as Maya and Seth were left to manage the split ends of their parents' divorce by themselves, many parents shut down two-way communication with their children during and after a divorce, leading to possible long-term problems that can last into adulthood.

> When my dad suddenly passed away in 2003, my first thought from the depths of my grief was, *Now they'll never get back together.* My father's death hit me pretty hard. Years later, I realized that I was grieving not only the loss of my father but the loss of my family. Something I had never been allowed to grieve or even acknowledge for many years.
>
> —*Forty-six-year-old (age eleven at the time of divorce)*

Keep in mind that your kids are also going through a divorce. They feel their own acute pain, grief, and sense of loss. For them, there is an even greater fear of abandonment and rejection because they do not understand how the divorce will affect their lives. Unlike adults, they are totally dependent. **Children feel that if their parents can exit or be pushed out, what certainty do they have that they won't also find**

themselves on the outside looking in? Their world feels torn in ways that parents often do not stop to consider. If you don't check in to find out what they need, or if your children are not comfortable expressing their concerns, you can't know the meaning of their loss. Take charge and confidently engage your children, reminding yourself that **the impact of divorce on your children is in your hands.**

In the Divorce Study, the most blatant discrepancy between the experiences of parents and children going through a divorce was that parents think they have communicated with their kids and met their children's needs. But there was a huge disparity between what parents perceive that their children experience and what their children report. **The Study showed that 51 percent of divorced parents said they spoke with their children and believed that they had met their needs, yet 87 percent of children reported they had no one to talk to about their feelings during the divorce.**

What Kids Need When Learning About Their Parents' Divorce

Not communicating sensitively about this major transition is devastating to your children and sets a poor precedent for family life to follow. **Children need to feel that they are part of the changes occurring in their family so they can feel safe to process their feelings.** You can help your children in age-appropriate ways by maintaining an open line of communication with them. During divorce, your children need constructive direction to vent their distress. Remember Ariana's drumming or her ripping notebook? In addition to enabling your children to share their thoughts, provide means for them to release tension, play, and be together with you—from taking a walk to playing a game of basketball. Your children's interests, like their favorite sports or television shows, resonate with their particular needs. To be supportive and attentive during the transition, it's helpful to structure responsive activities that speak in their terms. Communication occurs through words, body language, action, inaction, play, and events. You will know when they feel bonded to you in this process because of the deeper connection and certainty you all feel.

You set the tone for what your children can expect by the way you initiate the discussion of divorce. If you develop awareness of your children's needs and struggles, they will be encouraged to open up. If you are honest and open, you may even discover that you deepen your bond with your children because you have walked with them in their darkest hours—and yours as well. The most important message to communicate to them is that **the failure of your marriage does not mean the family and the children's own relationships are doomed.** By making this point and providing a stable, supportive, healthy relationship, you confirm this promise: *it's going to be okay.* By being with them, you demonstrate the power of a truly loving relationship, and you prepare your children to feel competent in close relationships with you and with others in their lives.

Once you have had that difficult first conversation announcing the divorce, you may think that the cat is out of the bag and you don't have to follow up on the impact of this conversation. In fact, the work is just beginning. Children in the Divorce Study expressed intensely negative experiences and emotions that characterized their lives after learning of their parents' divorce. **The words *agony, hurt, anger, pain, heartache, shock,* and *sadness* frequently described their emotions. Sixty-five percent of children in the Divorce Study described powerful, negative emotions in reaction to their parents' divorce.**

As parents, we want to be sure to accommodate our children's particular responses to the changes in their lives. When I have this discussion with divorcing parents in my practice, it's not unusual for them to minimize the impact on their children. They seem to be reassuring themselves that things are all right by explaining, "Most families experience divorce," "All my kids' friends have divorced parents," or "At least my kids will only go through one divorce . . . hopefully." Parents understandably struggle, and, unfortunately, they sometimes deny recognition of their children's feelings because of their own confusion and guilt. Such comments convey that they do not see their own children in front of them. (We'll discuss this more in the next chapter.)

Much of the pain children feel stems from the minimizing and emotional abandonment from parents as they try to cope with the divorce themselves. Parents who accept and work through the painful reality of their situation return to their children with sensitivity and a commitment to parent appropriately. There's a tremendous difference between situations where kids are, in effect, told to deny the impact of divorce and those in which parents and children deal with the realities.

During their parents' divorce, children are still in the midst of important developmental tasks, such as identifying with their parents, bonding, and learning boundaries. Remember—we must be available to serve as responsible parents and not be engulfed by the consuming aspects of divorce, sacrificing our most precious blessings. Otherwise, our kids will miss these invaluable life lessons.

Discussions with your kids about changes that may affect them confirm their sense that you understand and care—that you "get it." You understand that this is not just your family that is dissolving, but that their family is changing as well. In response, kids will more willingly share further insights about their experiences and feelings and participate in reshaping the family. The decision of divorce does not need to be unwieldy. Unintended damage that squashes your children's feelings, and your children themselves, can be avoided by responding directly to their concerns.

Through active engagement, you can respond to their feelings of loss as well as their fears. By being a positive role model for them—reinforcing self-control, practicing self-observation, and sharing their concerns—you can build an enduring relationship that gives your child a strong foundation from which to thrive.

Parental Recommendations

Five Basic Steps to Support Your Children During Divorce

Parents can have a powerful and positive impact on their children by being in tune with their interactions during divorce. Here are five basic supports to help your children through this process.

1. *Listen, love, and communicate.* Anticipate that divorce will have a significant effect on your children, and engage them to learn what they feel and what they need. Each child processes divorce differently. For example, remember how Ariana ruminated about her future, and how Seth calculated the improbability of divorce given Internet statistics? Take time to attend to and examine your child's unique response to the divorce, without going into irrelevant detail. Parents have an understandable but un-attuned tendency to share their thoughts about the divorce and use their children as sounding boards. Be attuned to your children's needs— not just your own—by responding with love.

2. *Answer their questions.* The average child will reasonably want to know what divorce means for him or her. Assure your kids that they will be safe, protected, and loved. Be ready to provide details that will assuage anxiety, and respond to your kids' emotions, questions, and need for clear detail.

3. *Self-observe: be aware of your feelings, thoughts, and words.* You will have specific feelings about your divorce and your former spouse that are not appropriate to share with your children. When these feelings are triggered, it's important to remember that the worst position for your kids is witnessing these fiery interactions and feeling as though they're in the middle of the two people who created them. To prevent this, discuss facts and refrain from making negative comments about the other parent. Acknowledge your sadness and distress after prioritizing your children's needs

and responding to their feelings and concerns. Ultimately, you need to retain your parenting role. (You will learn effective strategies for parenting during divorce in the next chapter.)

4. *Seek counseling.* Effective mental health providers can be a blessing in helping you and your children sort out troubling thoughts and emotions. Finding the right clinician, however, can be a challenge. You and your children don't need a warm body that sits but does not help; rather, you need an attentive caretaker to whom both you and your kids can openly relate. Your children need and deserve quality care, and, in this situation, you have an important role in providing the right guidance to your children in the absence of a suitable therapist. However, both you and your children need your own space to vent and process what's happening. If these needs are met, there will be fewer scars.

5. *Be your children's compass.* Children always need a compass (values and directions that lead them) and supportive, inviting, and loving guidance. Parents need to provide warm and caring support. Divorce is devastating for children when they feel alone, replaced, or supplanted. They need you more than ever; be there for them, and provide them with solid direction.

Above all else, make an effort to recognize your children's feelings and confusion. Your presence and attention confirm that you are still there for them, regardless of the familial changes. The most frightening anxiety for kids is that they are being cast out into the world, alone. In your words and through your behavior, assure them that this won't happen. You know your children's temperaments and demeanors better than anyone. *You will need to keep parenting through the divorce and well afterward*—it was your promise to your children when you brought them into this world. This means creating time regularly to talk to them about their concerns, fears, dreams, and wishes.

I know through my own experience with my children and through my clinical practice that when you meet your children's needs during divorce, you will secure the foundation for their well-being during this overwhelming time and beyond.

In chapter 2, you will learn approaches for managing stressful situations and suggestions so that you don't transfer your stress onto your children.

Chapter 2

MANAGE EMOTIONS AND STORMY SITUATIONS

Our marriage was not healthy. In order to be the best mom I could be, I needed to get healthy, which could only be done with my now ex-husband out of the home. I had to learn to set boundaries and raise my expectations of myself and my ex. When he began making poor choices and decisions over and over again, I realized I had to be a good example for my daughter, and allowing his behavior to continue wasn't the sort of example I wanted her to have when she was old enough to begin dating. Over the years, my mantra has been "Make good choices and decisions." I had to start with myself. . . . Choosing to stay with him was not healthy and not a good choice or decision.

—PARENT (MARRIED FOURTEEN YEARS)

Parental Oversight 2

Divorcing and divorced parents often react from deeply emotional places, rather than using the rational parts of their brains, and may find themselves unable to communicate effectively with each other. Driven by these emotions, parents often engage in battles in the presence of their children, neglecting to attend to their children's needs and expecting their children to manage the upheaval of divorce. Here are some of the consequences of not managing emotions.

Both of my parents weren't listening. The children became invisible. There was only shouting and screaming. My parents never understood their children. They were very selfish. Therefore, I kept everything to myself. I thought it was easier because I didn't want outsiders to start talking about my family.

—*Twenty-year-old (age three at the time of divorce)*

Not to sound too cynical but if you were to read a book on how to parent your children through a divorce, my parents did the *exact* opposite. We were dragged in and out of custody hearings. My mom only spoke negatively about my father (plus labeled him as "being like that side of the family," which had a profound impact). We were told lies about my father to try to create stronger impact when we were in court. My mom played a victim and let her children rise to being adults when we should have never been put in those situations. My mom even told me that I was conceived when he brutally raped her. . . . Need I go on?

—*Forty-two-year-old (age six at the time of divorce)*

It seemed to be an unspoken rule that this was an adult thing and none of it should have been my concern. No one ever talked with us about how we felt.

—*Fifty-seven-year-old (age thirteen at the time of divorce)*

Cindy was only fifteen years old when she became my patient. She had become suicidal during her parents' divorce proceedings. She was an only child, and she was mortified by the battles between her parents. So saddened by the breakup of her family, she told me that she cried herself to sleep nearly every night.

Cindy's parents rarely asked about her feelings. She felt that there was no time or place for her to express how the divorce affected her. She characterized her parents as "oblivious" to the impact the divorce was having on her; she claimed they were too busy fighting with each other and attending to their own interests to recognize that she was in the room.

Like most teens, Cindy was managing her own challenges of high school, dating, academics, and developing into her own person. With the onset of her parents' divorce, her world was turned upside down: "I didn't know where I was living, much less where or when I was going to go somewhere, who my parents really were, what they were up to next, or what was in store for me from week to week."

An attractive girl, Cindy had lost interest in relationships but eventually agreed to date a persistent upperclassman. When she worked up the courage to share with him her pain over her parents' divorce, he shut down and tuned her out. "He really had only one thing on his mind," she said.

When I asked her how she felt when he ran off, Cindy burst out crying: "I feel real bad. It seems that I'm either ignored or used by everyone. I feel like trash," she told me.

What if Cindy's parents had put aside their grievances and recognized her feelings about the divorce? What would have been different if they had been there for her, making sure she didn't feel abandoned, alone, or *worse*, responsible for the chaos in their lives? Parents often don't behave their best during a divorce; their fight-or-flight instincts come into play in a way that makes them forget the bigger picture: raising healthy children. They often lack the ability to recognize when they are reacting from a fearful instinct, not realizing that they can take steps to bring themselves and their children back into the world of the rational.

The time of divorce is critical for parents to turn things around, put their children first, and be there for them so their children won't feel lost. Even though parents may be aggrieved, children still need to play, feel joy, remain connected, and engage in positive, healthy activities. They need their parents to be actively present and available, even more than they were before the divorce. That's why, in this chapter, we will show how parents can handle their emotions in constructive ways that ultimately benefit the entire family. But first, let's explore why and how divorcing parents react destructively during the trauma of divorce.

BRENDON AND CARA'S STORY: PARENT EXPERIENCES IN THE THROES OF DIVORCE

It's not surprising that in the "he said, she said" stories of divorce, reality is presented very differently depending on who is doing the telling. Children often live within these yo-yo realities of their parents. Here's how ex-spouses Brendon and Cara individually report the intense emotions of their family story at the time of their divorce.

Brendon

As a devoted dad, I made it a point to be home when my kids finished school. However, Cara became increasingly impossible. She wanted me to work a second job, yelled whenever the kids made loud noises, and criticized everyone and everything. Because of our constant bickering, I suggested that Cara and I take a break for a few weeks. I offered to stay with my parents so that we could take some space and then restart. I couldn't take Cara's constant misery much longer, and I couldn't stand seeing our four small children frozen in their tracks during her outbursts.

When I came back to the house, armed with flowers and candy, and inspired by the idea of a new start, she had changed all of the locks. I couldn't get into my own home! At the time, three of our four children were in middle school. They are now all in high school. Cara had manipulated them so that they saw me as a dangerous monster. They are so afraid of me that they don't even participate in weekend, court-ordered visitations. Cara even told me that our children want to change their last name to her maiden name. She even concocted a restraining order against me based on her lies to keep me away from the kids. She won't let them speak to me, even on the phone. She ignores my calls, unplugs the phone, or creates excuses about why the kids can't talk with me. I find meaning in my family and being with our kids. Cara has done everything to keep me from them and uses our children to hurt me. She has destroyed my life.

Cara has a lot of anger. One time, she threw dishes at me. She told me to stop pushing to see the kids. She likes to give orders and see others jump through her hoops. I know I can't live with her, but I want to be with my kids.

Cara

I see my best qualities as kindness and caring. My worst quality is getting involved with my ex, Brendon. Brendon was physically, sexually, and emotionally abusive throughout the marriage. He even forced me into sex when the kids were around. They are afraid of him, though I'm not sure that they would remember his raping me after all this time. He appeared to be sober, but I was never sure what he was up to as he was always on the phone and not with the family.

Everyone knows that he's lazy and doesn't like to work. My kids don't want to talk with him on the phone because he torments them about seeing him. I would tell him to get another job, and he would say, "Why don't you get a job?" as if raising four children is not a full-time job in itself. I listen in on their conversations with their dad because I don't want him to hurt them the way he hurt me. He didn't know how to be a husband or a father. Even with the boys, he never tossed around a football, went fishing, or spent time with them. They were very disappointed that they never had a real dad.

He would take my money and spend it on his silly gambling aspirations or to try to win the lottery. He's a loser. He took food away from our table. He never bought presents for the kids that they enjoyed. He doesn't know how to talk to them. Sometimes, I would take them to visitations at his home, but he wasn't even there. His silly letters would say things, like, "You're a great kid! I know you'll have a great game," or "year," or whatever. How could he make these statements when he doesn't even know who they are? It's just stupid! He was always late to all of their games, but even when he was there, he was gabbing with other men or women or talking on the phone—not watching the kids.

He's a failure as a man! He's not a positive influence in their lives. To protect them from his negativity and his dangerousness, I want to get a restraining order so that he won't see the kids again.

Amid the battle raging between Brendon and Cara, do you recall that there are four children in this story? How do you think they're managing this warfare? Frequently, the flames of hostility between parents in divorce burn the children. For safety, children retreat into their own worlds. Though each side claims the children's best interest is his or her rationale for the divorce, children are often kept silent as the process goes on around them. The high emotion of the situation causes parents to forget to ask the kinds of questions we determined in chapter 1 are important:

- What are the children feeling?
- What can we do to help them?
- Who's paying attention to their real needs?

Some reactions from children who suffered similar situations follow.

I went from a straight-A student to barely passing, and I don't think my parents even noticed. There was too much going on. I started smoking cigarettes and pot, and drinking. My older siblings were also doing it. In fact, that's how they got me to be quiet.

—Forty-eight-year-old (age twelve at the time of divorce)

They were always wrapped up in their own world before the divorce. I was like an accessory at many times to them. They couldn't even handle their own problems, which even at the age of eight and nine I could plainly see. Trust me that when they battled each other, talking to them about my feelings just became more ammunition for them to use against each other.

—Twenty-eight-year-old (age eight at the time of divorce)

From reading these testimonials and Brendon and Cara's story, we get the picture of intense distress that the children suffered. Brendon and Cara's four children—like many kids who experience divorce—must have felt replaced by a seemingly more important battle. The majority of children in the Divorce Study described this common theme. Children stated that they felt as if the prominence of the divorce displaced their role in the family and that their own feelings were depreciated as their parents dealt with their own emotions. Though both Brendon and Cara acknowledged their four children when telling their stories—as do most parents undergoing a divorce—children are often relegated to secondary status and used as "ammunition" or "pawns" in an emotional battle.

In the Divorce Study, children consistently claimed that their parents were absorbed in conflict. While the isolation left them sad, children revealed that the most disruptive part of the divorce was the agony of witnessing their parents fighting. Also, the Divorce Study found that **38 percent of children claimed what hurt them most during the divorce was their parents not involving them or caring for them in the process.**

Do We Know What We're Saying?

Figure 1. Which Brain Are We Drawing Upon?

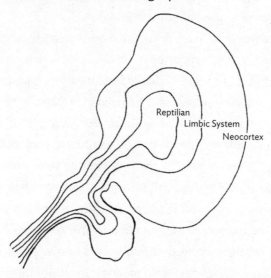

Reptilian
Limbic System
Neocortex

Region of the Brain	Developed	Functions
1. Reptilian	500 million years ago	• Breathing, heart rate, swallowing • Fight-or-flight response
2. Limbic	150 million years ago	• Emotional drives and responses
3. Neocortex	2–3 million years ago	• Learning and memory • Complex language skills • Logical capacities, abstract thought • Imagination and consciousness

Why do fighting parents react the way they do? Neuroscientists identify three distinct layers of the human brain that have evolved over the past 500 million years. Therefore, the brain is not one functioning structure but three, called the *triune brain*. The oldest layer of the brain is called the *reptilian brain*, which first appeared in fish nearly 500 million years ago. This deepest layer concerns itself with survival functions (breathing, heart rate, and swallowing) and the fight-or-flight response (what we do reflexively when we perceive something that feels life-threatening).

The middle layer of the brain is called the *limbic brain*, which governs our emotional drives and responses (like the fear you may feel when you think your spouse is in danger or other emotions you experience because he or she is late coming home). Appearing first in mammals, this area records memories and is the seat of emotions.

The neocortex layer of the brain is the most recently evolved layer and the most complex. The neocortex is what makes us human and involves learning, complex language skills, logical capacities, abstract thought, imagination, and consciousness. The neocortex permits us to take control with our higher-functioning skills. For example, if your spouse makes a comment that feels harsh, you would use your rational capacities (your neocortex) to ask, "Is there something that is upsetting you?" Whereas your limbic system might trigger an emotional reaction that would cause you to respond in anger. By using your higher-functioning skills via the neocortex, you engage in effective communication, clarify the root cause of the perceived difficulty, and resolve problems.

In a marriage, parents seek to engage rationally through their neocortexes—though they don't reference it that way. Triggers from unresolved situations in the past may spark visceral reactions (potentially limbic or even reptilian based) that are autonomic, or automatic, responses. These behaviors may require repair from past experiences or injuries. Sometimes these matters may be referred to as the marriage partner's "personal baggage."

> When I was thirty, I asked my dad why he did not love me. He told me that he could not stand the sight of me because I reminded him too much of my mom, and he hated her. I changed my last name that day.
>
> —Forty-five-year-old (age two at the time of divorce)

> I believe it is a good thing that they no longer have to see mom get angry and shout. I was incapable of keeping it in, even if I knew deep down that my kids should not be witnessing my breakdowns.
>
> —Parent (married thirteen years)

While seemingly unrelated current issues can stir historical issues, regular emotional sparring occurs during divorce because of emotional upheaval, creating a stressful environment in the home by limbic reactivity. When couples converse effectively, they often do so logically and rationally, using the neocortex. During arguments, emotional triggers are drawn, and the limbic and reptilian layers are activated, so the argument escalates.

An intact couple can recognize a need for repair after an argument, and they are able to communicate in a manner to preserve their bond. Conversely, divorcing couples have predominant limbic and reptilian engagement rather than neocortical, and they communicate less effectively. The presence of marital aggression can predict negative marriage outcomes, and, likewise, social support predicts marriage stability.[1]

THE GOOD FIGHT

When drawing upon your neocortex, you recognize when you and others constructively manage disagreements. Engaging only emotionally usually leaves us all where we began (or even further apart): agitated and disconnected. We know that our children may *hear* our instructions about how to relate constructively to others when we guide their behavior, but **nothing is a better teaching guide than our own actions.** It's often difficult to communicate from the neocortex without both parties engaged; however, keep in mind that rational exchanges that repair emotional issues defuse the toxicity of divorce for both parents, and they especially help kids. Here is the difference between parenting with *neocortex engagement* and parenting without it:

My parents always made sure to not say negative things about each other in our presence and were in communication when they needed to be. If they had an argument, we never knew about it. Divorce is not a defining factor in my life, and really hasn't changed who I am today. Maybe I am one of the lucky ones that it did not really affect due to having responsible parents.

—Twenty-six-year-old (age four at the time of divorce)

I am a carbon copy of both parents to a T. I mirror them. I am them. They taught me how to be dysfunctional to the best of my ability. Finally, they succeeded in teaching me something. I hate my life. It has no meaning or direction, goals or spirituality—just nightmares, horrible memories with physical scars, triggers, depression, anxiety, and panic attacks. It has been a lifetime of mental, physical, emotional problems and medications.

—Forty-four-year-old (age nine at the time of divorce)

Loving parents do not intend to function outside of the neocortex brain in order to undermine their spouses, yet these same parents, during divorce, tend to function in the limbic or reptilian brain. When you fight in these strata of the brain—especially in the presence of your children—you create a harmful environment. The rules of fighting in the limbic and reptilian arenas are visceral, pernicious, and violent. Such behavior puts your children at risk.

- Which part of the brain do you think Brendon and Cara were using?
- In your divorce, can you identify times of more cerebral functioning, as opposed to limbic and primitive activation, that helped support your kids in the past?

When we say divorce gets crazy, it's because there is often substantially less rational functioning and more primitive behavior. Depending on whether the relationship is amicable and civil or contentious and adversarial, children are exposed to both frightening examples and potentially traumatic experiences because of behaviors not stemming from our higher-functioning brains. Some situations are so severe that children are no longer able to recognize the parents they once felt they knew.

PETER AND JENNY'S STORY

Peter and Jenny had a storybook wedding. They had the support of their large families and were personally successful. Peter was an accountant, and Jenny was a third-grade teacher. Married for eight years, Peter and Jenny had two boys, a six-year-old and a four-year-old. Their boys were healthy and energetic, and both boys were diagnosed with attention deficit disorder (ADD). This storybook American couple was very active socially and looked distinctly fulfilled by external standards.

Inside the home, however, Peter developed a growing jealousy of Jenny, who sought to get in better shape. She went to the gym daily and participated in exercise classes. Peter began feeling isolated from Jenny, since he was either at work or on child duty. Their sex life had dwindled, and couples' counseling didn't improve their communication. Peter was convinced that Jenny was having an affair, so he hired a private investigator.

Soon after, Peter believed that his anxieties were confirmed. While Peter had no direct evidence, he tracked phone calls from different men who Jenny later explained were friends. She insisted the calls held no significance.

From Jenny's perspective, their marriage was becoming less and less fulfilling. She found Peter's notion of family confining and believed that nonsexual, friendly relationships with both men and women were essential to keeping her life interesting. When the investigator presented Peter with photos of Jenny having coffee and lunch with different men, laughing, and staying out after the time that she had promised to be home, Peter met his limit and filed for divorce. This was not the marriage Peter had envisioned.

Peter was not about to surrender his financial holdings or his children.

He asked the court for full custody, claiming that Jenny was an unfit mother. He further claimed that his youngest son had been sexually molested by one of Jenny's friends.

Jenny was shocked by Peter's action and overwhelmed by his claim for custody. She was also bewildered by the accusation of sexual abuse of their son.

Peter was granted temporary custody of the children, and court drama ensued. Jenny was initially granted supervised visitation, and over time, successfully earned visitation during the course of the three-year divorce proceedings. However, after the boys came home, Peter brought them to the hospital, claiming that the youngest child had been sexually abused and implicating Jenny's new boyfriend as the perpetrator.

Hospital records of the boy confirmed that the boy was sexually violated. Jenny's lawyer, suspicious of Peter's potential manipulations, had directed Jenny to have the boys examined before returning them to their father. The pediatrician confirmed that the boys were healthy and had enjoyed an excellent visit with their mother, without any incidents.

Had the parents lost all judgment? Was the mother or her boyfriend abusing these kids? Or was the abuser the father himself? This outrageous situation remains unresolved and in litigation—yet the tragedy of the children's situation seems overshadowed by the contentious parental battle.

Do you feel that your world has been turned inside out? How did this storybook family turn into a new version of the film *The War of the Roses*? (This 1989 classic American black comedy tells the story of how the idyllic marriage of a wealthy, seemingly perfect couple falls apart through an outrageous, embittering divorce.) Such tragedies as the movie depicts occur all too often in the world of divorce. If you feel that you are in the midst of one of these "crazy" situations, move very carefully, with your head on straight—full throttle neocortex. Following is an example of what might happen if things get out of control:

> My mother repeatedly told me my father did not want me. De-
> pending on how much liquor she had had, the stories became

uglier: He thought I was ugly; he wanted to put me in an orphan-age, etc. Probably not true, but still very hurtful to a child.

—Sixty-one-year-old (an infant at the time of divorce)

While the details differ, divorce battles with serious damage to the children are not uncommon. Divorces get ugly, and people can find themselves stopping short of nothing to bring the other person down. Actual divorce is more shocking and alarming than any screenwriter can imagine. You may be living out one of these dramas at this very moment. When your ex enters the picture, do you find yourself in a sudden down-pour of frightening emotions? Then be cautious; you may be descending into the unstable realm below the neocortex.

I hope these situations don't resonate with you. Yet the trauma of divorce knows no bounds. Situations can snowball out of control. Our children need us to maintain control of our emotions so they can assimilate to the changes of divorce, whether relatively civil or highly acrimonious. Boundaries provide structure for a strong, healthy, confident engagement. Each of us can do his or her part to establish healthy boundaries, particularly in the turmoil of divorce, to assure order. This means maintaining our roles as parents as much as possible, supporting our children in their age-appropriate activities and behaviors, and providing experiences and settings for our children to experience their lives as kids.

Therefore, parents must avoid getting caught up in the web of chaos that can erode boundaries, as you'll see demonstrated in the next story. While you may need to fasten your seat belt for the bumpy ride of your divorce, remember that there is no lesson greater than the behavior you model for your children.

BRENDA'S STORY

Brenda, an attorney married for seven years to a highly successful technology CEO, had two sets of twins. Financially stable with substantial resources, she and her husband employed both a nanny and a housekeeper full-time. No doubt the demands of her legal work felt all-consuming. Despite her many positive achievements, Brenda's lack of emotional fulfillment led her to connect with another man.

In therapy, Brenda often anticipated lines that she would not cross; then, she'd find herself violating her own standards. Before long, she was in a sexual relationship with Chuck, a fellow attorney, and struggling to manage the "perfect" world that she had created with her husband. Though both Brenda's and Chuck's families knew each other, Brenda and Chuck spent considerable time creating opportunities to get together alone—often, out of town. They asked, "Should we end our marriages since we've found the love of our lives?" When Chuck announced that his marriage was ending, his three sons were reportedly blindsided.

Brenda and Chuck were riding a runaway train, but Brenda was struggling to get off it. In therapy, she explained that her behavior was the result of her parents' own relationship nightmare, and that she had never known "true love" before she met Chuck.

Lost in the conflict were Brenda's and Chuck's children. Driven by their limbic brains and immersed in meeting their own emotional needs, the adults neglected to consider the impact that their behavior had on their sons and daughters.

It's difficult to pretend that we can walk in another's shoes, much less that we can fairly judge another's actions; however, we can't raise a family effectively by pushing boundaries to seek our own answers at the expense of others.

MARITAL RESPONSIBILITY

Direction in Life

When we have children, they are understandably the center of the home. Their well-being requires attention and care. Effective parenting necessitates direction and structure in the home and grappling with our commitments by communicating and engaging healthily with our partners. When parents do not impart these messages and actions in their lives and to their children, the very definitions of *mother* and *father* are compromised. Parents are no longer leaders, and the home is without direction and order. In the case of my teenage patient Cindy, Brenda's twins, and Chuck's boys, the parents are essentially on leave. The children end up paying the price for their parents' poor decisions. When parents have no direction, children often fail to develop purpose. Because the parents do not know what they want to do and are not doing what they need to do in their roles, the children are at risk as the parents instill uncertainty and confusion. There are no compasses to share. In my role as a psychologist, I attended empathically to the needs of Brenda and Chuck, who struggled with their unfulfilled emotional needs in their marriages. Yet we also addressed the needs of their children, for whom Brenda and Chuck accepted parenting roles but were not prepared for the "front-burner" responsibility of parenting: love as sacrifice. Many children in the Divorce Study echoed such experiences:

> There was so much dysfunction that involved alcoholism and rage that I perceived as my father's fault. I thought that his absence would make the drinking and rage stop and that my mom would have a better relationship with my sister and me. That was not the case. My mother continued drinking and partying and directing her rage toward me, which caused me to think I was losing my mind.
>
> —*Forty-three-year-old (age ten at the time of divorce)*

Sacrifice in Marriage and the Family

Parents have personal needs—component parts woven into the fabric of the home life. At the same time, words like *commitment* and *sacrifice* carry a weight beyond our personal needs for those to whom we have made a commitment. If these words do not manifest in actions, our children will be compromised. Who is tending to the children in these stories? The other parent? A babysitter? When your son has football practice or your daughter has a soccer game, as a parent you are brought to a similar kind of moral dilemma as that of Brenda and Chuck about whose needs prevail. Will you sacrifice a spa treatment or a golf game because parenting means being present, first and foremost, in your children's lives, going to their games and nurturing their development? Or will you indulge yourself? The following comment from an adult child of divorce expresses how children are often left alone to make sense of their parents' choices that don't include them:

> Do you stay together for the sake of the kids? Does divorce impact grown children? Both my parents have moved on and have significant others who have families that they are now committed to. I ultimately want them to be happy; but it feels unfair that they have sacrificed my happiness for their own, and I try (most days successfully) to just love them and accept their choices.
>
> —Forty-one-year-old (age twenty-three at the time of divorce)

STOP THE FIGHTING—ESPECIALLY IN FRONT OF YOUR KIDS

Previously, I referred to intact homes with parents who are essentially divorced—that is, parents who retain their formal contracts but for all intents and purposes live as though they are divorced. In these households, children endure the same destructive forces as children exposed to divorce. Parents who regularly fight create the same harmful climate for their children. Some researchers report that divorce *per se* is not detrimental to children, but rather it is parental fighting that creates the greatest harm and is the single strongest predictor of long-term damage.[2] Although numerous intervening variables and theories about the impact of divorce abound, most researchers agree on one basic point:

parental fighting is unquestionably damaging to children. Answers from both parents and children in the Divorce Study confirmed that divorce is more damaging for the family than anticipated.

> I was stuck in the middle way too often by my father. He was very manipulative and tried to use me in the middle to get to my mother. He also said hurtful things about her that were very inappropriate for him to say to me.
>
> —*Twenty-four-year-old (age twelve at the time of divorce)*

Fighting can easily provoke limbic and primitive engagements of the brain. It can take many forms—from name-calling, insults, abandonment, and physical aggression, such as hitting and pushing, to silent reactions, such as sulking and conceding or giving in to someone's demands in order to stop the conflict.[3] When these behaviors occur, parents can heal the psychological damage they can cause in children. Just as you would treat a physical wound, you want to attend to the emotional needs of your children. Just as you would not send your children to play in the dirt with an open wound, parents should not re-traumatize their children by triggering anxiety-inducing behaviors with their arguments. The sheer volume of poorly managed divorce cases makes social agencies' interventions against these actions not only challenging but also unlikely. The demand far exceeds any intervention that the Department of Children and Family Services could address.

Psychologist E. Mark Cummings, a professor at the University of Notre Dame in South Bend, Indiana, conducted research on the impact of parental fighting on children. He concluded, "If parents show positive emotion in the middle of fighting, if they say nice things to each other or are affectionate . . . it changes how kids see conflict."[4] Cummings's research highlights how conflict affects children's sense of emotional security about the family. This research highlights the importance of parents functioning from the cerebral brain (the neocortex)—using words to communicate emotions constructively.

Cummings's coleader, Patrick T. Davies at the University of Rochester, conducted three studies of children in different age groups (nine- to eighteen-year-olds, kindergarteners, and a long-term study on six-year-olds). He concluded that parental conflict wasn't a problem for children when parents resolved the conflict, but when conflict remained open, the children responded with anxiety and depression.[5]

The Dirty Dozen: Behaviors to Guard Against

Parents do not seek to distress their children. Nonetheless, the following twelve actions frequently emerge during divorce and are among the most agonizing experiences for kids. These actions, supported by what children reported in the Divorce Study, are often blind spots for parents overwhelmed by the divorce process. Each deprives children of the normal experiences of childhood and burdens them with negative emotions they do not have the capacity to process. Recognizing the Dirty Dozen and avoiding them is essential to freeing your children from the burden of divorce.

1. *Don't put kids in the middle.* When parents cannot communicate with each other directly and their divorce becomes increasingly contentious, they may resort to making their children take sides. During a divorce, children are under extraordinary strain to make sense of a redefined relationship with their parents. Keep children away from adult decision-making or from making them serve as the parents' mouthpiece.
2. *Don't use kids to fight the battle.* Be vigilant against involving your children in the marital fight. It is inappropriate to threaten to withhold visitation rights or solicit or bribe your children to side with you against the other parent.
3. *Don't treat kids as property.* Kids often get relegated to property status—as things to be won or lost or shuffled between homes— when parents address the fate of their children during divorce.

This is not only demeaning to the children but also diminishes their personal significance and semblance of family for them.

4. *Don't reveal legal details.* Legal actions are often imposing and contentious, escalating the anxiety and despair of children. Parents should work conscientiously to shield children from legal issues that invariably heighten the exposure of loss and pain when children become exposed to the "fighting arena" of court.

5. *Don't disclose secrets about your spouse.* Children should not be privy to the personal details of their parents' lives. Divorce usually results from unacceptable or disturbing allegations about parents, such as affairs. Private information and character evaluations should be kept from children; such information may be debilitating and unfair to the parent who seeks to retain a positive relationship with his or her child.

6. *Don't "split."* In order to co-parent, parents must communicate effectively, using their neocortex brains. If they cannot provide a united stance, regardless of their differences, two types of splitting can occur. First, in an effort to enlist the child's support, a parent may present himself or herself as the good parent while portraying the other parent as dishonorable or deficient (a subject addressed more carefully in chapter 3). Second, a child may learn to play parents against each other for his or her secondary gains. Both forms of splitting threaten the stability of the parent-child relationship.

7. *Don't engage in "guilting."* When parents plead their case, play the victim, or describe to a child the unfair treatment they suffered, they infuse guilt into the scenario. Demands and pleas for sympathy, no matter how subtle or indirect, place children in the unfair position of feeling sorry for their parents. Children may even assume responsibility for causing the divorce, which can be emotionally damaging.

8. *Don't suffocate.* Some parents are so overly involved in their children's lives that they monitor them beyond appropriate

boundaries, seeking to counter the difficulty of divorce through inappropriate physical or emotional closeness. Suffocating behaviors—such as over-monitoring children and not permitting them privacy—limit kids' ability to establish their own spaces, create their own identities, and negotiate their relationships with their parents.

9. *Don't project a personal agenda onto your children.* Children need to be given the space to develop their own thoughts, views, and conclusions about the divorce process. Rather than permitting their children this exploration, divorcing parents often project their own agendas, trying to direct and correct their children's thoughts, in an attempt to shape their kids' views.

10. *Don't engage in marital conflict in front of the kids.* Whether a conflict is explosive or passive, physical or verbal, children need to be spared exposure to their parents' fights. Parents are most helpful when they demonstrate mature channeling of their feelings and disagreements through constructive conversations.

11. *Don't use kids as the support system.* It's a problem whenever parents turn to kids for comfort, emotional reassurance, companionship, or the fulfillment of roles that a spouse would normally fill. A dependent parent who sends the backward message that "Mom or Dad depends on you for survival" puts extreme pressure on the children. Nature created the parent-child relationship the other way around, and it needs to stay that way. This dynamic is also known as "emotional incest," as this creates similar psychological damage as physically violating a child.

12. *Don't alienate.* Alienation results from barraging children with negative information about the other parent, or distancing oneself from the children in order to meet one's own needs. Children require relationships with both parents to enrich their trust in the value of relationships. Only in situations when a child's well-being is threatened by contact with a parent should restrictions be initiated.

Recommending a list of dos and don'ts for good parenting during divorce may seem totally unrealistic. It's not reasonable to expect that things will always operate systematically and in a controlled manner during divorce. In the face of direct and public attacks or a spouse who is out of control, you may feel that the Dirty Dozen establishes a standard that is beyond reasonable and requires superhuman powers. Be that as it may, when children are directly embroiled in the drama of divorce, minimize and become mindful of your child's exposure to troubling behavior. You can't control anyone else; all *you* need is to follow the maxim that I found practicable in my own divorce: "Do your best, and leave the rest to God"—an affirmation that also happens to be a tenet of Alcoholics Anonymous.[6]

A Word About Managing Extreme Situations

Controlling your children's exposure to improprieties is sometimes impossible. I have been counsel to many disturbing situations where children were overexposed to their parents' unseemly behaviors. They have walked in on a parent's romantic activity with another adult, experienced the humiliating behavior of parents under the influence of drugs or alcohol, read their parent's inappropriate e-mails to someone other than his or her spouse, and witnessed lewd or illegal actions by a parent.

In these situations, guide your children to a therapist or spiritual counselor. Your children may need the opportunity to express their confusion, mixed feelings, hurt, and anger. While you are an informed and resourceful source of valued support, you are also the "other" parent, and your child may become protective of and overly invested in you.

Your kids need guidance and trusting relationships to manage the special challenges of stormy situations. Be sure to reflect on your actions to assess whether or not your behaviors exhibit good judgment, prudence, and honor. Your children will be best served by experiencing your support through your presence and assurance over collusion against your spouse.

Parental Recommendations

Parents know that quality communication is in the best interest of the children and can enhance everyone's lives. Yet situations when a man feels he has just been "taken to the cleaners" during a divorce, or when a woman learns that her husband has had a mistress and a double life, can make rational communication very complicated. Parents embroiled in their breakup can have difficulty finding common ground. Divorcing and divorced parents may find basic communication complicated because they are not simply rational exchanges. The following self-observation exercises walk you through being a better communicator with your former spouse—and the tips work just as well in conversations with your children too.

Self-Observation Exercises

Before you start any discussion, make a conscious effort to keep your emotions in check and engage your neocortex. Here are some tips that can help you navigate the conversation:

1. Take a few deep breaths before diving in. Slowly inhale and exhale at least eight times.
2. Center yourself. As you work to conscientiously clear any negative thoughts from your head, your mental state will become clearer and your heart will open to being more receptive to what the other person has to say.
3. Focus on being present and aware. Tune in to what the other person is expressing to you and how he or she is feeling—not on your own thoughts and emotions.
4. Afterward, take a moment to think about the interaction as if you were observing from above. If you witness yourself contaminating the conversation with your own agenda and negativity, or responding in a hostile manner, work on being more self-aware and constructive.

5. Track your thoughts and behaviors by writing them down. If these contaminating actions continue to occur, consider discussing them with your own therapist.

If you seek therapy, focus on addressing and changing behaviors that result in your lack of presence, because they can be destructive to your children. Keep up with your self-observation exercises too. And, if you're daring, record and listen to the way you behave with your kids. You may find there are more things you want to address with your therapist so you can be the positive influence your children need during this time.

Twelve Ways to Ease the Stress

Divorce is all-consuming. It invades all aspects of one's life—physical, emotional, spiritual, and social. These twelve strategies will help you navigate the turmoil, making you a more engaged parent and allowing you to communicate more rationally with your spouse and children.

1. *Acknowledge negative feelings.* First, identify what you're feeling. (Psychologists identify six primary emotions: happy, sad, afraid, surprised, angry, and disgusted.) Then make a plan to work through your negative feelings. Bottling up your negative emotions only creates a ticking time bomb.

   I kept things to myself. I wrote in poetry books for years about the mental and physical abuse of my mother. We were living a fake life on the outside and on the inside of our home was constant turmoil and pain.
   —*Thirty-seven-year-old (age thirteen at the time of divorce)*

   By modeling for your children how to work through your emotions, you set a healthy example for helping them deal with their own negative feelings constructively. Boys in particular often act out in anger during a divorce. Internalizing their pain, girls may develop eating disorders or cutting behavior (or other forms of self-harm) either to release them from feeling pain or to allow them to feel something in the midst of numbness.[7] But do not label your child as explosive or having a behavioral problem when he or she is merely reacting to the upheaval of your divorce.

Help your children find constructive avenues for their emotions. This doesn't have to cost a penny. Playing a pick-up game of basketball, baking together, taking a walk, or going for a run can be very effective coping mechanisms. This redirection of energy into positive, constructive behaviors can have lasting benefits on your children's coping skills.

As I previously mentioned, after she learned that a divorce was to ensue, my seven-year-old daughter began banging a large pot with a spoon. It was most likely an effective way for her to release the stress and anger she was feeling and couldn't express. However, her actions spoke to me. You'll recall that I bought her a used drum set so she could express herself when she felt the need. Though she chose to take drum lessons and learn more, this activity was her stress release.

2. *Have fun!* The power of laughter is a well-documented antidote to illness.[8] Have fun with your kids by relaxing together, dancing, going out with friends, watching a movie at home, or playing with the dog. Understandably, play and fun may be awkward at first without the other parent, who is absent because of the divorce, but consider establishing new rituals with your kids. Try going out for ice cream (my favorite) or go to a sports game or concert together. While you don't want to fill every second of your children's day with distractions, you may be pleasantly surprised when they welcome opportunities to spend time with you. Don't deny yourselves this joy, and don't feel guilty for having fun.

3. *Exercise.* It's rare that young children don't want to play, go bowling, go skating, or do something physical. Pleasurable activities

together—whether they're moderate or physically challenging— release stress and strengthen emotional bonds. Some of the most meaningful conversations fathers have with their sons happen on the basketball court or while tossing a football back and forth. A simple walk is one of the easiest activities for most of us to do. With older kids, you can discover activities that you may have missed when they were younger. Ask them to introduce you to some of their favorite activities. The ancient Greeks, like Socrates and Aristotle, were onto something: the *peripatetic* school, or talking while walking, is indeed productive and therapeutic. Great ideas and heartfelt experiences have the chance to marinate when you're out taking a simple stroll through the park. Shared pleasant time together is the ticket.

I can attest that during my divorce, the routine walks I took with my children became an invaluable tradition that we continue to this day. They'd open up and provide more detail as we took our walk around the neighborhood pond and shared time together. I learned about school and their dreams, thoughts, questions, and personal doubts. During these times when we simply walked, no subject was off limits. With the same ideal in mind, we all enrolled in a local gym. Exercising together allowed us to do something with one another that also had the added benefit of being an all-around healthy activity—and provided more time for laughs.

4. *Prioritize self-care.* Massage, pampering, and the various spa arts, like Reiki or a chiropractic adjustment, work to release tension in the muscles as well as enhance relaxation. Making time for this type of self-care may be out of your budget, but you can arrange more affordable experiences, such as swimming, massaging your child, or taking a nap. The goal is to shift from the mental stress of the divorce into a pleasant state of consciousness—one that allows you to breathe, think, center, and access happiness. Self-care can also include identifying your needs versus your wants,

scheduling time to unwind, or incorporating hobbies that can reduce stress, like cooking or learning a new skill.

5. *Take a hot bath.* Hot water can loosen tight muscles and provide calm, soothing relaxation. Take a dip in your gym's hot tub or use your tub at home—accented with pleasant music and candles—to create a relaxing ambiance in which you can decompress and de-stress. Though you take such breaks alone, the fact that you prioritize them may show your child the importance of setting aside your preoccupations and introducing positive feelings and emotions into your life.

6. *Breathe!* Stress-reduction programs based on improved breathing techniques document just how much basic breathing can calm the entire body and counter the daily pressures that can endanger our health—something so essential that the divorce steals from you without you recognizing it. Breathing-based meditation and longevity breathing provide documented health benefits and immediate relaxation. By simply taking control of your breathing—inhaling and exhaling slowly, increasing your lung capacity with continued breaths, and envisioning positive imagery—you release that which is not useful. You'll also relax your muscles and restore clearer thinking. Additionally, from this newfound calm, you can discover the life within you as a person who is not running in a tailspin but who is in control and centered. This is one of the most inexpensive and readily available tools to counter stress.

7. *Take a break.* The stress of divorce can come from being embroiled in court proceedings and entangled in emotionally charged battles with your former spouse, while simultaneously working double-time in your single parenting. You may feel bombarded by a continuous flow of tasks, regrets, and mixed feelings. There is value in refusing to give in to the flight-or-fight response and simply stopping and taking a break. You may be surprised with how receptive your kids will be to join you in doing nothing!

8. *Nurture your body.* The chaos of divorce can easily lead to a change in sleep schedules and dietary habits. You may find yourself eating and drinking things that provide quick energy bursts or comfort rather than the healthy food your body needs. You may be more susceptible to fast foods or illicit substances that weaken the body because they appear to be a convenient form of self-care. At the same time, the regimen of preparing good meals—or the motivation for conscientiously preparing meals—may remind you of times with your spouse that you wish to avoid. Though you should cut yourself some slack because you will undoubtedly need to adjust, your body needs solid rest in order to manage the new challenges.

   While you do not want to harp on good behaviors or cause more complaints, you can model the right choices for your children. "Make the right choices" is a mantra you should establish across the board. In the face of depression, children may be prone to submit to the quick fixes of drugs and alcohol. Head off these downward spirals with clear instructions and preventive guidance. Cooking meals together may be one ritual that you can initiate to counter the negative influences.

9. *Develop friendships.* In college, I purchased a plaque that best illustrated my relationship with my one true friend. It depicted two overlapping circles and read, *A friend doubles your joys and divides your sorrows.* That is exactly how I feel about this friend to this day. I still use the words from this plaque to assess my friendship with others. Am I serving as a true friend by dividing my friend's sorrows? Is he or she my real friend by doubling my joys?

   Caring relationships generate joy and love. It is critical to have these important relationships so that we may help our children discern the characteristics of genuine friendship.

   Sometimes, children encounter problematic challenges in their friendships that are a direct result of their parents' divorce. At a time when they need true friends, they may find their options limited, and they may turn to anyone to get their needs met. Your children will need your counsel and guidance in these times. Be sure you are there for them to help them steer the course and make good decisions.

10. *Access all your emotions appropriately and know that it's okay to cry.* Sometimes, the pain is so great that you cannot cry, and other times, you cannot stop crying. This is often the case for children, though young boys and men, in particular, are often ashamed of visibly expressing their emotions. Let them know that real men *do* cry and that crying is a natural part of life, regardless of gender. Crying frees emotions that cause stress and releases potentially harmful chemicals that build up. You undoubtedly feel better after crying—whether it's during the joy of a touching moment, the birth of a child, a wondrous ending to a story, or after a miserable situation that caused you to break down. Several studies confirm that people who are "internalizers"—those who do not express their emotions—suffer greater physical and emotional distress and illnesses than those who allow themselves to release pent-up emotion.[9]

If you feel the need to cry, make room for those tears; they deserve your attention. It's okay to cry, and you should feel free to express this natural emotional outlet in the presence of your children. At the same time, be aware of its impact and discuss these moments with your children, who may experience your tears as frightening. Keep in mind that if you find yourself constantly on the verge of tears, you may want to consider professional help to address the source of your feelings. Remember: your children are not your therapists.

11. *Consider meditation.* Meditation has been around for more than five thousand years. It has been ignored by the scientifically minded for decades, but today you can't pick up a journal in any medical specialty that does not report on the benefits of

various forms of meditation. Meditation focuses on deepening spiritual and religious objectives and can lead to greater self-awareness, as with today's popular "mindfulness meditation."[10] Mindfulness meditation seeks to clear the mind and requires that you do nothing—often very challenging for busy people living in the modern world. The goal is not to give in to distractions but to remain focused, either on a spiritual task or on nothing in particular, and to observe yourself and learn who you are.

One of the potential benefits of divorce is that the challenge may lead you to ask deeper questions about your life and the way in which you want to guide your future. It is easy to neglect these types of personal and philosophical questions in the course of our busy lives. While meditation is quieting, it is also deeply enriching and can lead to great strides in self-discovery.

12. *Deepen your spiritual life.* The philosopher Søren Kierkegaard said that prayer changes the nature of the one who prays.[11] Man, as a natural being, cannot know God, who is supernatural. But prayer is a medium that enables the natural to engage the supernatural. Prayer offers a dialogue between God and the one who prays. A relationship with God has the power to transform a single heart or an entire nation. While many people pray with words, it is the prayer of the heart—when it is motivated, passionate, believing, and engaging—that is truly transformative. In the depths of the darkness of divorce, prayer can shed light on the unknown.

I know of no greater hope and power than prayer. Prayer transforms distrust to hope, confusion to possibility, and uncertainty to knowledge. Prayer dispels the darkness of divorce and opens us to the light of life.

Successfully navigating stormy situations requires a delicate balance where you remain available and communicate honestly. Yet it is important to retain appropriate boundaries in your relationship. You can best help your children by retaining your parental position in the relationship and supporting your children. Your ability to maintain boundaries in the parent-child relationship as it evolves during divorce is the topic of the next chapter.

Chapter 3

SUSTAIN YOUR PARENTAL ROLE

I believe that if your marriage interferes with your parenting skills in the sense that both parents cannot focus on their children and provide them the loving care and attention that they need and deserve, then divorce might be the best solution. I do not agree that people should stay because of the kids. It's actually selfish to think that way. Kids would prefer to have both parents focused on them separately than living under the same roof with constant fights, no affection, and no structure.

—PARENT (MARRIED FOURTEEN YEARS)

Parental Oversight 3

The confusion and stress of divorce can blur boundaries and cause parents to relate inappropriately to their children. You or your ex may compete in currying favor with your children, becoming more lenient, spoiling them, or creating an environment where your children can manipulate you. You may also lean heavily on your children for emotional support, effectively switching roles as you become dependent on your children.

> My father remarried almost right away. My mother shut down and, in a sense, stopped parenting for a long time. My father would say the most hurtful, inappropriate things about my mother. My

mother would talk to me like I was an adult. She would share info with me that I didn't need to know. No one tried to protect us and reassure us that everything was okay. Visitation with my father was not consistent on his part. He would take my brother and not me. He treated me like I was my mother. I could go on for days . . .

—*Twenty-eight-year-old (age seven at the time of divorce)*

Divorced parents should always remember that they are divorcing their partners, not their children. Even if their children are older, they are still affected in many ways. A parent should not open up about all their feelings with their children, even if they are older. Parents should, rather, get a therapist and give their emotional baggage to them.

—*Twenty-nine-year-old (age twenty-six at the time of divorce)*

Initially, my dad started to tell me about his sex life with other women. He told me about what he bought at sex shops, his dating life, etc., and this was before they were officially divorced!

—*Twenty-seven-year-old (age twenty at the time of divorce)*

Adrian was a graduate student who came to see me about his difficulties with women. Within a short time, it became clear that his difficulties were rooted in the fact that his mother had depended on him for support because of her volatile relationship with his disloyal father.

"My dad cheated on my mom for thirteen years, until she finally had enough and asked for a divorce," Adrian told me. "She treated me like I was her therapist with no regard for how I was affected by the material she shared."

Adrian's mother disparaged his father, and men in general, throughout Adrian's childhood. She even took her son along when she staked out hotel rooms to catch his father with other women. Adrian recalled riding in the car with his mom on many nights as she complained to him about how his father did not honor their marriage.

Yet Adrian was conflicted. He grew to hate his father, but at the same time, he yearned for his father to be there for him "like a normal dad." Once his parents were divorced, Adrian said his mother made it clear that she didn't want him or his sister visiting their father, even though she said they could if they wanted to. This created a no-win situation for Adrian. He needed his father, but Adrian did not want him in his life; and his mother gave mixed messages that left him feeling he would be disrespecting her if he visited his father.

"In time, I actually developed a longing for my dad but couldn't ever express it to her," he said. "She should have talked to her friends or a therapist instead of involving me. I wish she had left me alone."

Adrian said his mother put him through "emotional torture." He had no one to turn to as a child because his father was "emotionally unavailable" and never tried to bond with him. Plus, he found his situation at home too embarrassing to share with others.

As Adrian grew older, his mother's behavior only worsened. After the divorce, she began bringing other men into their home and engaging in sex with them. She made no effort to hide her personal life. Adrian said, "She even walked into my room half-naked after having sex with someone. She would stay out to all hours of the night, and I stayed up worrying about her."

Adrian was robbed of his childhood by his mother's psychological abuse. With the boundaries blurred significantly, his needs were ignored. His mother shared information with him that was suitable only for an adult. She was overly dependent on her son to the point that he suffered emotional trauma that has had a long-term, adverse effect on his ability to form positive and healthy relationships with women.

Reversing the child and parent roles is certainly a form of *emotional* child abuse. This chapter zeroes in on how both you and your child can retain your appropriate parent-child roles and confront situations that tear away at the fiber of these boundaries. Children are not only robbed of their childhoods but also damaged into adulthood because the lack of boundaries and attention to the needs of the developing child leads to confusion.[1] The parent who is most present can sometimes influence children in a manner that results in role confusion with the parent who is less involved, whether the other parent chooses not to take on responsibility, loses custody, or visits infrequently. This leads to complicated relationships, as in the following story of the Simmons family.

THE SIMMONS FAMILY STORY

When Stephen and Emily Simmons ended their twenty-year marriage, they quickly modeled classic "good parent/bad parent" roles for their children. After Emily caught Stephen in romantic exchanges on his cell phone, Stephen admitted to having had a long-term affair. He had not been a hands-on father throughout the lives of his four children, all of whom were teenagers at the time of the divorce. But during the custody battle, Stephen began showering his children with expensive gifts and fancy vacations. He even offered to finance their college educations, which was not required by the divorce settlement. Emily felt that losing his "father" badge motivated Stephen to stake his claim on the kids.

One of the enticements Stephen created for his sons was a hideaway he called "the ultimate man cave." There he hosted his sons and their friends and dispensed illegal substances. Stephen used such gatherings to segue into introducing discussions with his sons about the new woman in his life.

Initially, the Simmons children were wary and suspicious of their father's motives and newfound interest in their lives, but he slowly began winning their support through gifts, trips, and cash. Though all the children were skeptical of their father, stronger disagreements developed between the sons and the daughters about whether to accept their father's largesse—particularly as the girls had been in the dark about the man cave. The struggle between their father's newfound generosity and their feelings of loyalty toward their mother began to tear at the bonds between the siblings.

Stephen defended his gifts to the children as good-faith expressions of his love and for smoothing the transition brought on by the divorce. He openly acknowledged his absence in their lives, explaining that he was the breadwinner of the family and needed to travel. However, he was now back!

Emily felt that Stephen's actions cast her as the bad parent because she always maintained a firm parenting posture and was not about to compete for her children's favor by enticing them with gifts or special trips. Increasingly, the boys wanted to stay at their dad's house, but she thought this stemmed from the boys' need for him. She was unaware of the man cave and never considered that Stephen might be introducing them to illegal behavior.

At one point, Emily smelled alcohol and marijuana on the boys' clothing. When she confronted her sons, they firmly denied any substance use and reassured her that they "would never do that kind of stuff." Because she was not used to doubting them, and the boys had always confided in her, she didn't think they would lie to her.

Emily's concerns turned from caution to alarm, however, when a local minister called her and confronted her after his children had come home intoxicated after a party with her sons in the basement of *her* home. The neighbor-minister said that Emily's sons encouraged his children to join in the drinking. Furious about their behavior, she confronted her sons, who took full responsibility. They admitted that they were learning things in the man cave that could have serious consequences. This wake-up call resulted in the sons telling their father that they appreciated his desire to get to know them better, but that they thought the man cave was leading to harmful repercussions. At this point, Emily decided she had little choice but to take Stephen to court to limit his time with the children.

Seven Divorce Pitfalls

The following seven pitfalls terminate healthy family relationships and introduce complicated dynamics into a child's life. They highlight the common trap of blurring the lines between parent and child, which can affect not only that relationship but also the children's ability to build successful relationships with others.

1. The Good Cop/Bad Cop Challenge

As introduced in the Simmonses' story, Emily and Stephen epitomize the good cop/bad cop model of parenting, which paints one parent as the fun-loving, adventurous, and permissive friend and the other as the strict, boring disciplinarian. I've seen this dynamic play out many times with divorced couples whom I counsel, as they compete for their children's affection instead of serving as responsible parents. Stephen explained that he was aiding in his kids' post-divorce adjustment by lavishing them with gifts. Unfortunately, his efforts confused his children and ultimately put them at risk. They also put his ex-wife in a very difficult position as she tried to maintain discipline and strong values in her home.

Statistics indicate that more than 25 percent of children are raised by single parents.[2] Some of these children have visitation with noncustodial parents who struggle to establish a meaningful bond with their kids. The good-cop role is especially appealing to the noncustodial parents because it can be enticing to children. Noncustodial parents often struggle with how to effectively express their parenting role, and they frequently shed the time-tested qualities of firm and loving guidance and resort to the role of playmate and friend. These stand-in efforts fail to serve either child or parent.

The good-cop parenting dynamic is inappropriate because children require clear boundaries to internalize discipline. The good-cop option can also reinforce damaging behaviors, as in Stephen's allowance of illegal substances for his underage sons. Kids are willing magnets for excessive privilege and rewards and can learn to manipulate these circumstances to their initial advantage—and ultimate detriment.

> I was shuttled back and forth between states and ultimately made the choice to stay with my father all through junior high and high school. He never enforced any rules and let me get away with a lot. I got into the party scene and drugs at a very early age. I do not think a twelve-year-old should be able to decide where to live. It should have been decided based on who had the best environment for a child to grow up and have supervision. My father tried, but with his work schedule I ended up raising myself; and I did not make the best choices for myself. . . . I needed someone there to guide me, and I didn't have that.
>
> —*Thirty-one-year-old (age four at the time of divorce)*

When children see their parents split (something they don't enjoy), they are prone to engage in splitting behaviors themselves for immediate gratification (something they find attractive and pleasant). These behaviors frequently occur at a critical time in a child's physical and cognitive development. Children require firm and loving support to avoid misdirection, ideally from *authoritative parents*. The authoritative parenting style supports a child's growth through healthy guidance, despite the child's preference for the path of least resistance. Research confirms that *permissive parenting*, or parenting that is *laissez-faire*, results in children who are not well regulated, perform poorly in school, and experience problems with authority.[3] It's worth mentioning that considerable research has found two other parenting styles to be detrimental. The first is the *authoritarian parenting* style that produces children who behave obediently but who rank low socially, in both self-esteem and confidence; these children also tend to feel unhappy in response to oppressive parenting. The other is *uninvolved parenting* that results in kids feeling unwanted and insignificant, creating children with the poorest outcomes in personal development. Ultimately, children seek authoritative parenting guides, which lead to maturity and leadership. Your parenting style should be shaped with consideration to healthy guidelines that meet your children's specific needs.

2. Winning a Child's Favor

Noncustodial parents use gifts and special privileges in an effort to create positive responses from their children and to gain more access to them, especially when their time together is limited to weekends or less. A more manipulative motive may be retaliation against the ex-spouse. By creating disruption, noncustodial parents may feel they are getting back at their exes, undoing their former spouses' efforts. When parents try to win favor with their children and abandon an authoritative posture, they create an imbalance in their role as a supporting parent. They shift to a deficient—permissive or uninvolved—parenting style, focusing on their own agenda and not on the best interests of their children.

3. Splitting

Splitting occurs when parents destroy the unity of those in control and enable children to pit parents against each other. The Simmons boys were enticed into this place following Stephen's invitation to the man cave. Research makes it clear that children seek firm and loving support from a parent who demonstrates the authoritative parenting style.[4] Of course, splitting occurs not only through a division between parents but also as a further division within the family that intensifies during the breakdown of loss, structure, and values.

4. "Parentification"

My parents told me way too much information. I became an adult when they split up. I was aware of every hidden flaw each parent had, and I felt betrayed and abandoned. It set me up for adulthood in the worst way because I was forced to grow up quick and take care of my parents. I did everything wrong and allowed people to treat me bad. I closed myself off from friends.

—*Twenty-six-year-old (age twelve at the time of divorce)*

Children like Adrian, who was forced into acting like his mother's therapist, get *parentified* when they are placed into parenting roles. As a result, such children feel as though they need to take on the parental roles to rein in their parents. During the chaos of divorce—when children need more guidance, support, and direction than ever—parents often do not enforce rules or provide solid direction essential for guiding their children's development.

Here are five simple steps you can take to create the types of boundaries your children need for healthy development:

1. Clarify expectations.
2. Discuss the rules and regulations of your home.
3. Follow through with reasonable consequences for violating house rules.
4. Uphold respect for the other parent.
5. Retain your parenting role through sound leadership.

5. Power Imbalance

A shift in power from the parents to the children often occurs during a divorce. Ultimately, such a shift has a destructive impact on the children and the home environment. In the Simmons family, Stephen became friends with his sons. He tried to win the children over by literally buying their affection. These actions do not establish genuine authority but instead feign power, which children do not respect as legitimate. Though everyone should have appropriate power consistent with his or her position in a family, during a divorce parents who need to fill these roles often do not retain their power as the roles deteriorate. This is either because of formal court decisions or because parents do not act responsibly in their parental roles. When parents do not execute their parenting responsibility, children are placed in positions of judgment or given power inappropriate for children their age. Parents can often feel disempowered by the divorce, the actions of their former spouses, the children, the custody arrangement, or their own inaction.

> I know I rushed into another relationship; and I don't know where that relationship will lead. But my children are important to me. I will do anything for them. I was just tired of parenting alone, work-ing, and dealing with all the problems by myself—and there were many. I have suffered from bipolar disorder all of my life. Dealing with the kids alone really has taken a toll on my mental status.
>
> —*Parent (married nineteen years)*

Children need parents to be parents. Although taking control may be tempting for children, and they may manipulate situations because the authority structure weakens and breaks down during divorce, par-ents remain in the position to stay in charge and retain their function. In doing so, they avoid confiding in their children, sharing inappro-priate information with them, or placing adult responsibilities on them. Although families will regroup and redefine their roles during the divorce process, parents do not have to forfeit their role of how they empower their children. As resources change, a redefinition of roles and responsi-bilities will understandably occur.

Even when you feel disempowered by a court decision or a child's resistance to recognizing your authority, **you can remain true to your role and do what's right based on your moral compass**.

> When I explain car insurance is the law, and her father states he doesn't have any, again I am pointing out how her father is not doing what he is supposed to do. This is not my intent, but it is my job as a parent to teach her right from wrong. This co-parenting with an ex-spouse is tough for everyone.
>
> —*Parent (married four and a half years)*

6. New Liaisons

The lack of awareness for parents—particularly those leaving a marriage for another partner—is not recognizing the disturbing impact relational changes have on children. Stephen's effort to talk with his boys about women in the man cave was a transparent attempt to introduce his new girlfriend into their lives. In this process, for the boys, their mother was replaced—a confusing dynamic that understandably stirred resistance from Stephen's sons. Stephen's action was further confirmation of the family's dissolution that the children had not yet worked through. For a child in a divorcing family who was not given the opportunity to make adjustments, new liaisons are perceived as interlopers and met with opposition. Forcing such engagements is highly disruptive.

> I feel lonelier because I can't trust anyone anymore. I can't even trust my parents. . . . Never in my life have I been this angry, this upset, even aggressive. I still feel like I want to smash someone with a baseball bat multiple times until my anger is over.
> —*Twenty-five-year-old (age twenty-three at the time of divorce)*

Adults may make such changes more easily than children because they are directing the change, and they are not the one losing a parent. But children require time to accept the change in their parents' roles—to recognize them as separated and emotionally connected to other people. If you are seriously interested in another person, psychologists often recommend taking at least six months before introducing him or her to your children so as not to overwhelm them. Similarly, it is a mistake to parade different romantic interests before your children, particularly if they form attachments to these people; this can recapitulate loss. Keep in mind that you are forming a model of family life for your children's future.

7. Losing Continuity

During divorce, boundaries are often eliminated on many levels. Emily worked conscientiously to retain her persona with her children, supporting continuity with structure in the face of change. When we sustain continuity, children feel secure. This should not be executed rigidly and inflexibly, which can deny natural growth and development.

Emotional abuse is elusive; it does not usually leave physical scars. However, it is very damaging because it affects the way we think about ourselves, often crippling us with untruths and loss of self-confidence and self-esteem. **The Seven Common Pitfalls of Divorce must be avoided because they create potential opportunities for emotional child abuse by causing confusion and blurring boundaries.** This may sound like a strong indictment, but succumbing to these pitfalls can deprive children of the essential nurturing they need to thrive.

PARENTAL RECOMMENDATIONS

Securing Your Parental Role

Consider the following questions to see whether you are maintaining your parental role during and after your divorce:

1. Do you sort out your intense emotional feelings with your children?
2. Do you consider your children to be your best friends?
3. Do you interrupt your children's social lives and integrate yourself with their friends?
4. Do you make your children feel responsible for your happiness?
5. Do you avoid activities with other adults apart from your children?
6. Do you sort out the details of your problems concerning your (ex-)spouse with your children rather than with another adult or professional?
7. Do you ask your children for advice about handling your (ex-)spouse?

x

Establishing and maintaining positive, healthy, and clear boundaries provides solid care for your children. Your answers to the aforementioned questions should be *no* across the board. If you find that you are reconstructing these questions so that you answer no, your boundaries are not as defined as they need to be.

In divorced and intact families alike, kids need their parents to be parents. For healthy development, strive to uphold these four principles of positive parenting:

1. *Maintain clear goals and values.* Focus on your models for guidance and direction in life, return to your spiritual supports, and redefine what is important and what provides meaning and definition to your life. This directs you and your children away from possible disorganization and diffusion to time-tested direction and values. I recall feeling extraordinary pressure at many times during my divorce. Again, my daily mantra became, "Do your best and leave the rest to God." I worked each day to communicate with my children that even if clouds are in the sky, this is a day like no other; let's not miss it. I encouraged them to make every breath count. In addition to our shared time together, I wrote brief, personal, positive notes to them every day—and they responded with their heartfelt reflections as well. I engineered positive discussions and identified inspirational activities, and we engaged in healthy, supportive activities together. There was lots of laughter (which my son specialized in providing through his shenanigans or his finds of humorous YouTube videos). Moreover, it was reaffirming to my children to see that though life might be hard, we were together, and we would all be fine if we made good decisions and worked at it. This bonded us! Our spiritual resources—through joint prayer, conversation, preparing meals together, playing together, and talking about our lives very practically—had reinforced our bond. Light appeared in the darkness. This is not to suggest that we didn't confront and

manage arguments, struggles, and problems, and it does not suggest that difficulties and misunderstandings did not occur, but it reflects the value system and positive orientation we embraced.

2. *Set clear expectations.* As a result of divorce, both children and parents may feel that the family has dissolved. This is not only unnecessary but also disastrous when it becomes the living reality for children. **Divorce is not an end to the family; it's a transition in the family's development.** Your ability to guide this process in a positive direction is essential for your children's well-being. Children need structure and support for their development; the family is an ideal matrix to support both the continuity and the direction. Redefine your expectations for your children in the developing family structure and assure them of their secure place by confirming that they find support in the family's changed situation. In the Simmons family, because Stephen was frequently traveling on business, the family had identified roles and a system Emily guided that seemed to functionally exist without Stephen. Their divorce caused a disruption in the system, as Stephen became "actively" involved. By contrast, Emily's structure provided a core of respect that ultimately prevailed, although it was shaken through the turmoil Stephen created. Parents going through a divorce often feel that "there's a hole in the bucket," as they bring emotional supplies to the family, which are drained through the complexities of daily living, including complicated schedules, multiple sets of rules, and inconsistency or lack of routine. To some extent, this may be part of the cost of divorce and a reason for you to work harder to maintain your family.

My father made sure we still had memories together, whether it was riding around on bicycles or having our annual movie night. It may not have been our ideal situation, but he gave it his all—the life he knew we deserved.

—*Eighteen-year-old (age seven at the time of divorce)*

3. *Discuss rules and regulations for your home and reasonable consequences and rewards.* When the boys lied to Emily and humiliated her with their actions, she implemented consequences. Emily believed that part of creating a good home was preparing her children to live in a just society. Similarly, by supporting and rewarding her children for their achievements, she helped them establish their personalities and clarify their goals in life. The home, even after divorce, must mirror a good society in order to create a positive vision for your children's future. Society includes rules, and, for Emily, it included the consequences for breaking those rules. Reasonable consequences render reasonable children. Do not forgo consequences, as you would not forgo rewards for your children's achievements. This is part of maintaining your parental role. **As the leader, you need to be clear about rules, rewards, and consequences in your household as the family takes on a new form.**

I have a lot of friends that lose it, and I did too for a while, but my mom is old school. She didn't take my crap. Though sometimes at night I would hear her cry and mourn, you would never know that anything was wrong. She handled it all and kept the three of us in line and on the straight and narrow. I know what my mom went through. She is the strongest person I know.

—*Twenty-year-old (age sixteen at the time of divorce)*

4. *Uphold respect for the other parent.* Acknowledging the value that both parents bring to their children's lives is critical during a divorce. Regardless of how complex the divorce might be, each parent usually seeks to maintain a parental relationship. You will make a personal determination of how the other parent fits into your life, but it is important that you permit your children to do the same for themselves. Otherwise, you will confuse your children and cause them to be conflicted about their parents' roles in their lives, as in the case of Adrian and his mother.

My mother and I had started to get closer as I became her confidante. I wasn't a daughter, but rather someone my mother
could vent to. When my mother started dating someone and
he moved in about one month after her divorce, I quickly had
to switch roles and start being an obedient daughter. It was
disastrous. I fought with my stepfather the whole time I lived
with them. My father had another baby with my stepmother;
and as a teenager I just wanted to hang out with my friends, but
I couldn't because we were expected to go to my dad's house
every Friday night through Sunday.

—Forty-year-old (age ten at the time of divorce)

When you align your objective and your ultimate principles—looking
into the eyes of your child and confirming in your mind that you are taking the best actions—you should know that you're doing your best. You
deserve to sleep well and know that you are doing what is right. This is
something you should be very proud of—especially in the midst of this
storm.

In chapter 4, we'll consider the impact of handing off your children
to others and how to negotiate time for your children and time for you.

Chapter 4

PROVIDE STABILITY
THROUGH NURTURANCE

Every situation is different, including family dynamics. But divorce changes kids.
Sometimes I do feel like we "killed" who they could or would have been. It forces
them to grow up in ways before they should have to. I deal with guilt . . . even seven
years later.

—PARENT (MARRIED ONE YEAR)

Parental Oversight 4

When children are moved from one home to another during a divorce, the effects can be disorienting: nurturing is compromised; routines, relationships, friendships, and childhoods are disrupted; and the perception of "home" is sacrificed. Threats to childhood stability also occur if you default on parental responsibilities and hand off your children to relatives, friends, teachers, programs, or therapists for primary caretaking.

> The home I grew up in eventually was sold and my parents moved away from my hometown. I had *no place* to call home. Home no longer existed and ties to my hometown were broken. . . . The

divorce was the end of innocence; and I launched into adulthood very quickly.

—*Forty-three-year-old (age eighteen at the time of divorce)*

I expressed the longing for a father figure, the empty feeling of not having him there, and the questions of why Daddy doesn't want me.

—*Twenty-three-year-old (age four at the time of divorce)*

When Darin began counseling with me, he focused primarily on his sexual dissatisfaction in his marriage. He had divorced after fourteen years in a passionless marriage. He had two daughters (Penny and Kayla) with his ex-wife. During his counseling sessions, Darin hardly discussed his children and their needs. His children did not appear to be much of a consideration for him both during and after his divorce.

Darin said he and his wife had married in their early twenties, thinking that it would bring them closer together, despite the lack of an intimate connection in their relationship. Both partners pursued relationships outside the marriage because neither found fulfillment with the other.

In sessions with Darin, I often asked about his daughters. He treated my inquiries about his children like unwanted interruptions. When the girls were supposed to be with him, he shuttled them off to his parents' home. Apparently, his ex-wife also had the girls living with her parents most of the time. This arrangement, Darin said, "gave them the space they all needed."

In a curious expression of concern for his children, he once suggested that boarding school might be the best option for Penny, "to help her get away from the constant moving around," and provide stability for her since his ex-wife was involved with a former high school boyfriend and because Penny complained about "not having a home." Penny was petrified at the thought of attending boarding school because it was just another form of rejection from her parents.

When I asked about his relationship with his daughters, Darin responded, "I see them every weekend for a few hours, pretty much like every father." Darin said, "The girls are doing fine." He concluded this because they did not complain except for the occasional protest about moving back and forth between homes, being away from their friends, and having difficulty participating in school activities because of their new visitation schedule. I suggested that he bring them in for a session so we could see how the breakup affected them. He agreed.

Penny and Kayla came to my office but never made it past the waiting room. They initially sat quietly and seemed very shy in the waiting area until I finally broke through their timidity by greeting them and asking about their music preferences. They became immediately animated and started talking about their favorite bands as well as a concert they hoped to attend.

As we were making a positive connection, I was about to invite them into my office when Darin interrupted. "Hey, Doc, there's something I really want to talk with you about. Can I see you first?"

I agreed, and Darin and I went into my office. He began to talk about his sexual anxiety with a woman he'd just met. He was so focused on his distress that I had to interrupt him to remind him that the girls were waiting in the lobby.

"I can bring them next time if we don't have time," he said, as if they weren't even there.

He continued to talk about his sexual issues, using up the entire session with his daughters sitting in the waiting room. When I went to say good-bye to them and asked them to come back for the next session, they hugged me and smiled. Darin never brought them back. When I asked why they didn't return, he said they were too busy.

Darin's situation is not unusual. Not only was he too preoccupied with his own concerns to address his children's needs, but that preoccupation also led him to pass off his parenting obligations to family members and other third parties. **The Divorce Study found that when parents responded to questions about their children's needs, they focused primarily on their own needs.**

I was going through so much myself that it was difficult to process my feelings, let alone theirs. Admittedly, I was very selfish during the course of my divorce, often putting my needs ahead of my children's.

—Parent (married nine years)

Parents often both consciously and unconsciously avoid and discount their parental responsibilities as they reenter the dating market, frequently handing off the children to grandparents or other relatives; or, in some cases, children are left to raise themselves. Additionally, the necessity for single parents to manage more than a full-time job to meet financial necessities can make access to their own children very limited. According to the Divorce Study, about 78 percent of children found someone other than their parents (or no one) helpful in managing their parents' divorce.

The core of your child's well-being comes from your sustaining nurturance. If you neglect to nurture your child, especially in the throes of divorce, the stability your child needs for healthy development may be threatened. Note the uncertainties described by children in the Divorce Study concerning their absent parents:

- "My parents keep dumping me on other people. Am I that much of a burden?"
- "Mom and Dad aren't around for me. Does this mean I am on my own?"
- "Does my parent's boyfriend or girlfriend mean more to them than me?"
- "Will this stranger comfort me better?"
- "How can I better comfort myself?"
- "Do my parents love me?"

From the Divorce Study, we see that Darin's daughters are not alone. Many parents displace or overlook the importance of nurturing their children in the aftermath of divorce, leading to long-term negative outcomes.

> They forgot they were still parents. They became so wrapped up in their new lives of dating and eventual remarriage that I was left alone a lot. There was even a Christmas that I had to spend with my married older sister because both of my parents were gone.
>
> —*Twenty-six-year-old (age twelve at the time of divorce)*

Darin's lack of attunement to his daughters' needs is disturbingly common. In fact, 57 percent of children from the Divorce Study reported receiving little help from their parents during the divorce process. Children often questioned their parents' care and involvement and the way they demonstrated limited parenting responsibility.

Parents need to ensure that their children are supported in their physical, emotional, and spiritual growth and cultivate care required for such development. For your children to thrive, they require *quality care* and *nurturance*, which are the foundation for a stable home life. Let's explore what nurturance means.

NURTURANCE: KEY FOR PROVIDING STABILITY

Nurturance occurs through your physical, emotional, and spiritual nourishing of your child; it is the formative requirement for raising healthy children. Parents often question the extent to which their children will be affected by their divorce without realizing that the two primary resources needed to raise healthy children are the parents' stability and support. As these two resources dissolve and fail to function during divorce, children are left with scarce nourishing supplies—which are required for cultivation of their development through the parents' physical, emotional, and spiritual care.

We know that children are vulnerable and fragile; their worlds are shaped by the sustenance they receive. Positive experiences of trust, engagement, and love encourage optimism, joy, and security; while negative experiences of disappointment, aloneness, and abandonment create doubt, defensiveness, and uncertainty.

Every one of us can look back on our lives and think of situations when we felt loved and situations when we felt neglected. We can each think of the warm hand of a loving parent or genuine friend that sustained us at a critical juncture; that person's belief in us led us to conquer a critical challenge. Similarly, we can recall individuals who disabled us, discouraged us, rejected us, and created barriers that closed doors, such that we abandoned our dreams.

My greatest fears were realized. My foundation was ripped out from under me. My foundation was both of my parents together. Even though I saw my dad whenever I wanted, and he lived close by, there was no scheduled visitation. So things that I know would never have happened if he lived there happened. Because my mom worked nights, we were on our own for a lot of hours—every day after school until 10 p.m. at night. I don't blame my mom for that; she had to work. Nor did I resent having to watch my younger siblings and care for them; but if my parents had stayed married, my mom would have been home, and we would have had the moral and parental guidance we needed. My stability was shaken, and I felt abandoned by my dad even though he did not abandon me. I felt he picked his new wife over my mom and us kids.

—*Forty-eight-year-old (age twelve at the time of divorce)*

They blamed me for everything. They blamed me for going to college. Then they blamed me for leaving after one year at school. I dropped out. I just didn't care. I gave up my dreams because my

parents blamed me. Now I am twenty years old and taking online
classes for business, which is not what I really want to do. I have
loans to pay for a school that I didn't even finish.
            —*Twenty-year-old (age sixteen at the time of divorce)*

Some psychologists argue that divorce has a positive effect on children, claiming it breeds resilience and feelings of achievement. Despite the
possibility of such positive outcomes, other studies reveal the opposite.[1]
For example, the Divorce Study found that only 35 percent of children felt
happy or normal upon learning of their families' dissolution, resulting in
the negative consequences that the respondents described. Another study,
conducted by the National Institute of Mental Health, found that infants
nurtured by families that were not intact were more likely to cry, fuss,
and become less engaged than infants of happy parents.[2]

Child development studies confirmed that there are critical pillars to
children's upbringing, such as one's health and well-being, safety, community and spiritual involvement, language and cognitive development,
social and emotional support systems, and, of course, love.[3]

We learn from the Divorce Study that when parents ignore the
impact of their children's living conditions after a divorce, children are
negatively affected. Children are left to navigate the world with a dysfunctional compass, transitioning from one home to another, forced to
adapt with an unpredictable outcome. Approximately 73 percent of children reported a familial upheaval as their greatest fear about the divorce,
according to the Divorce Study.

Sadly, these children often experience complications due to personal
deficits that make their own relationships and life engagements a lonely
struggle.

My "child" heart will forever be broken. The last couple of years it
has been even sadder for me because I do not have a relationship
with either of my parents. They refuse to hear my hurts. I still stay

in contact. But it feels like I am just pretending or that it is one-sided. I am happier when I have no contact with them.

—*Thirty-five-year-old (age twenty at the time of divorce)*

CHILDREN NEED NURTURING

For years in my classroom, I've used the metaphor of a seedling developing into a plant to describe how internal and external environmental nurturance parallels child growth and development.

Figure 2. Soil and Environment Nurturing Growth

Thriving Growth	Threatened Growth	Impaired Growth
		• Deficient parental support
	• Child left home alone	• Child manages self
• Loving family with sustaining bonds • Actively engaged physically, emotionally, spiritually • Nourished with quality care	• Limited financial and emotional support • Parents absent from meals • Parents not maintaining contact	• Parents miss visitations, don't call, are absent • Fighting constantly • Parents inattentive

Note that Figure A shows a flowering plant (child), firmly rooted, that flowers unimpeded. Figure B presents shading and rocks in the soil that block the development of the roots' growth. Figure C presents greater jeopardy through more environmental impingements that block light, including rocks in the soil that impede the plant's growth.

This metaphor shows how both plants and children seek light (which symbolizes inspiration and spirit), to which they are naturally drawn. This light produces fuel that drives growth toward their full potential. **Parents can best serve their children when they recognize the importance of assuring their children's access to light. They do this through introducing awakening of passion, a sense of purpose, meaning, and direction—the basis of moral and spiritual direction.** Every gardener, or parent, needs to consider the access that his or her seedlings, or children, have to light. When we help our children recognize that the power of light is available, and when we emphasize their need to embrace it, we awaken within them a sustaining resource for bonding and discovering their truth. This imparts a fundamental message of nourishment in parenting.

We can predict thriving development based on "light" and the access the seedlings (children) have to good soil (healthy settings), watering (regular care), and fertilizer (supports appropriate to the unique needs of the child).

Divorce almost unequivocally depletes supplies a child draws on for nurturing because of reduced time, resources, and competing tasks and roles of both children and parents. The good news is that this risk is not inescapable if parents recognize these problems, counter the detraction, and attend to the loss.

HOW TO PROVIDE NURTURANCE

In divorce, the task of nurturing becomes more complex because we have fewer resources and increased impediments, such as career demands, reduced finances, parental custody challenges, moving to another home, and more. When parents are able to focus on nurturing their children—despite the challenges created by divorce—stability is reasserted, children learn to feel assured and grow confident in their maturity—and parents are reinforced for their valiant endeavor.

Plants need light to thrive. Light is the spiritual resource that allows us to see every day as a new beginning and perceive the possibilities for one's self-growth. Whether that spirituality emerges from the optimism and energy of the parent; from engagement in the arts, sports, and nature; or through specific guidance in one of the great religious traditions of the world, parents serve as a catalyst for encouraging and nurturing this resource. This does not mean parents must deny their own personal struggle of divorce. Instead, they can find re-motivation when they **maintain perspective and recognize the blessing of their children and what they, too, are going through. By paying attention to what their children need to fully develop, parents may experience the power of the sacrifice of love with which they are entrusted.** Together, the parent and child may rediscover life's possibilities outside of the challenges created by divorce.

> I wasn't privy to most of their arguments. My mother was very calming and reassuring that we'd get through this. We were still a family.
> —*Thirty-four-year-old (age eighteen at the time of divorce)*

> My mother had to take me to a child psychologist because she couldn't leave me alone without me bawling loudly until she came to get me again. The psychologist concluded that I believed she needed me to function, and that she would miss me too much. It was because of him that my mother put me through drama classes outside of school—which eventually led to a drama scholarship to the only specialist arts high school in Western Australia. I had a lot of fun at that school. So maybe it turned out to be a positive experience after all?
> —*Twenty-two-year-old (age three months at the time of divorce)*

The light we all intrinsically seek and depend on is freely available. Our ability to receive light, however, may be limited by our inability to perceive it, if our vision is hindered by the circumstances of our past or our current environment. As parents, we have the responsibility to ourselves and our children to sustain the light that shapes our beings.

Removing contaminants or transplanting them to new, well-fertilized soil may provide the necessary environment for them to flourish. Like plants, we require healthy environments in order for positive change and substantial growth to occur. The yearning to survive and to seek the strength to thrive is inherent within us. Without healthy, positive, nurturing resources, children and parents alike may turn to unhealthy models to sustain themselves. Some fall into depression or develop dependencies that *feel* relieving or helpful, like substance abuse, as a way to ignore the pain or escape the loneliness they feel.

No life is perfect, and most of life is spent in growing toward some end, in some direction. Like plants, humans are organic, changing, and imperfect, yet they have the potential to be extraordinary. They may grow in light or in darkness. Parents are in the prime position to guide and enact changes. Children are more vulnerable and act more impulsively and less maturely. They require guidance when life becomes tragic.

I was sexually abused as a child for about five or six years. I never felt comfortable talking to my parents about it because they were so wrapped up in their lives. My father rarely ever said two words to me; and I was worried my mother would end up institutionalized if I told her. I turned to the wrong group of people and ended up sneaking out at night, abusing prescription drugs, and going to parties where drugs and alcohol were abundant. While I was eventually able to deal with the abuse, my mother only recently found out and my father still doesn't know.

—*Twenty-year-old (age fifteen at the time of divorce)*

I feel so guilty for not having made the right choices and perpetuating the cycle. Now I worry my children are not capable of making proper choices in their own personal lives. One son has never had a girlfriend and his brother has been questioning his sexuality (something I don't care about). I just worry they can't be in a relationship because I've damaged them somehow. I really think people underestimate the damaging effects divorce can have. I'm 47 and my brother is 44 and we both have difficulty to this day.

—*Forty-seven-year-old (age nine at the time of divorce)*

To take the analogy even further, we must remember that plants come in multiple varieties; growing in different seasons and in dissimilar conditions, their blossoms cover a spectrum of colors. A good gardener knows he cannot care for all his plants in the same way. Successfully growing roses by watering and fertilizing them in a particular way does not mean that carnations will grow equally well given the same treatment. Parents, like gardeners, best serve when they nurture the needs of their individual children and monitor the children's responses. The major point is that it is crucial to understand our children's unique qualities and to nurture them so their authentic potential blossoms.

MARK AND CHERYL'S STORY

Mark and Cheryl were given joint custody of their four adolescent sons even though they could not communicate on most matters. They frequently used the court as a forum to play out their ongoing marital battles, which continued to rage more than twelve years after their divorce. The boys resisted going to their father's home and expressed anger at being shuttled back and forth, away from their friends and preferred routines. They were especially resistant because their dad never responsibly participated in their lives, particularly as they began high school. In therapy, Cheryl told me that for years, the boys cried, threw their clothes around, and acted out both before and after visiting their father. She felt that Mark never wanted to take on the parenting responsibility for the boys but used joint custody to avoid paying child support.

The difficulties escalated when Mark developed a relationship with a woman, leading him to frequently cancel his time with the boys. Often, he picked them up and dropped them off with his parents or another relative, claiming that they needed to stay connected to his side of the family. The boys rebelled from being shuttled from place to place. Cheryl struggled to maintain structure in their lives, but the court-ordered custody arrangements thwarted her efforts.

Once the boys reached their teenage years, they used their father's house as an escape from their mother's disciplined home environment. Cheryl had remarried, and with the supportive efforts of her new husband, they attempted to rein in the boys. Although the boys accepted their stepfather, they claimed that their parents' divorce ruined their lives, and they used guilt as a method to mute and control their mother.

The four boys began going down a dangerous path of fighting in school, truancy, poor grades, drugs, and alcohol. The oldest son eventually came around as he developed an alliance with his successful stepfather and tried to serve as a role model for his brothers. Unfortunately, his success was limited. The two middle sons pitted their parents against each other and frequently acted out, while the youngest son had the most severe problems with substance use.

You would not expect a houseplant to survive if you moved it back and forth, weekly, from one setting to another. We wouldn't do this easily for a pet dog, cat, bird, or fish. Why is the same standard not true for our children? It's important to ask:

- What's the impact of continuously uprooting our children from one setting to another?
- Is it fair for the well-being of children if parents impose their equal legal claims and require that they live split existences?
- Whose needs are best met through such arrangements?
- How am I attending to the impact or toll that my children experience from the routine our parenting schedules require of them?
- Is the parenting schedule in the best interest of the children?

Supporting children during a divorce is very difficult, particularly when the homes and parental styles of parents and stepparents are managed differently (which will be discussed further in chapter 8). The decision to terminate the partnership and leadership of a home has huge ramifications for every child. Children are left asking which parent's rules they should follow. They also often wonder if there are different rules in different homes, or, "Do I really have a family anymore?" In these situations, splitting and boundary difficulties frequently intensify. Children feel empowered—to a fault, at times—by the diffusion and lack of order in their lives, as they knowingly and unknowingly participate in their new freedoms. You may wonder if there are other alternatives. Rather than letting such situations generate unwelcome crossroads by not attending to the consequences, it may be valuable to consider which of your responses in these situations best serves the interest of your children.

Cheryl was disempowered in her role as mother. Regardless of all her good intentions, her ex-husband successfully weakened her authority, making her feel powerless. The open-door policy Mark initiated permitted the boys to go to whichever house they chose, on demand, which resulted in the boys exploiting this freedom, leading to disorganization and aimlessness, paving their road to drug and alcohol abuse as coping mechanisms.

A stable setting is in the best interest of the children. While courts can find that they are between a rock and a hard place in determining which home is best for the children, this principle, more than serving shared parental rights and claims of the children, should guide the decision. It may be necessary to move your children between homes during and after the divorce, yet every effort should be made to provide stability and continuity for your children—including continuity of an authoritative parenting style in both homes. If this cannot be achieved, it is often in the children's best interest to choose a best setting, rather than have the children torn between incompatible environments. Parents can ease this transition by creating new family rituals to build bonds and ensure a sense of security for their children. These rituals can include eating and speaking together, playing together, creating activities where you all participate, and creating traditions that provide definition for *your* family. Engage with your children as active members of the home, and attend lovingly to their growth. This is how parents ensure their children's needs will be met so the children will not go elsewhere to fulfill these basic needs.

> My parents remarried three times; and we always moved around after each divorce. I went to twelve different schools by the time I graduated from high school, and moved fifteen times. My self-esteem was not present at all. I was picked on constantly!
> —*Forty-five-year-old (age six, eight, and twelve at the time of divorces)*

Find ways to stabilize your children's lives and to provide them with a sense of security. When your children feel unloved and uprooted, they are prone to rebel or try to manipulate the situation toward more favorable alternatives.[4] Their understandable resentment and anger from stressful living situations can trigger retaliatory actions that may result in long-term emotional and psychological problems. Every case is unique, but I caution parents to be sensitive and to put the welfare and needs of their children above their own needs and legal rights—a high virtue in the struggles and trenches of acrimonious separations.

Children in the Divorce Study commonly described feeling like "baggage" or "property" throughout the divorce process and its aftermath. Many children of divorce acknowledged that they abused the situation by taking on power that was inappropriate for children their age and splitting their parents for secondary gains. Although they felt some immediate gratification in such actions, this resulted in their development of dysfunctional relationships and their unpreparedness for adult life.

The court system often plays into this when dividing up children like property. The court would best serve children by considering the long-term impact of custody decisions for co-parents like Mark and Cheryl, who are unable to communicate and cooperate. While it is not possible to co-parent when parents do not communicate effectively, the court system, which is overburdened and unable to attune to the needs of the overwhelming number of divorce situations, often applies formulaic solutions to give both parents equal access to the children. This places children in nonhomogenous environments—settings with different parenting styles, values, rules, and traditions, which may be at odds with each other. Mark and Cheryl's boys were not nurtured in rich soil. When parents use the good-parent/bad-parent tactic (described in chapter 3) as leverage for personal gains or pressure their children to choose one parent over the other, serious consequences inevitably occur.

> I thought I would have to choose sides. I don't think there is any child of divorce who hasn't had to pick a side. Whether it is picking a side of who's right or wrong, or just who to live with. I didn't want my parents to hate me for not choosing them.
> —*Twenty-one-year-old (age eleven at the time of divorce)*

IS CONTINUOUS TRANSPLANTING IN THE BEST INTEREST OF THE CHILDREN?

In addition to the task of nurturing, the divorced parent carries another challenge related to the well-being and stability of his or her child: managing the responsibility of coordinating custody and visitation.

A common maxim of the court is that each parent has the right to access and be present for his or her children. Though this "right" is fair and equitable, what is the cost paid by children of divorce who move back and forth to accommodate parental visitation? Children described that they feel as though they are "pawns in a chess game" or "inanimate objects." How does the plant metaphor illustrate the impact weekly or bi-weekly visitation has on children? No gardener would recommend this process for the well-being of a plant. **Plants would not thrive with constant transplantation, yet we transplant children regularly between**

homes without accounting for the damage this creates. A gardener would take great care in managing a single transplantation of a plant out of concern that the plant could be damaged or its roots compromised, thus impinging on the plant's growth. Yet such adjustments are imposed on children, conveying the expectation that children should adjust, adapt, and perform, as if disordered lives for children of divorce are normal and reasonable. The effects are described in the following reports of children in the Divorce Study.

I do not remember much about what happened because I was so young. But I do remember one day living with my dad and the next moving without him.

—*Twenty-year-old (age four at the time of divorce)*

My world fell apart. It was surprising to me. All my friends' parents were still married; and I felt embarrassed. The wonderful life I thought I was living with—two parents, a home, church, the same friends I had for years—ended with me moving away from those friends in seventh grade, seeing my dad twice a month, living in an apartment, etc.

—*Twenty-five-year-old (age ten at the time of divorce)*

My dad packed us up literally in the middle of the night to move us from North Carolina back to Pennsylvania with the help of moving vans and relatives. My mom did not know he was going to do that. My mom would still come over after school before my dad would get home to help us a little and to visit us. I can only imagine how hard that was for her when she found the house empty one day and we were gone.

—*Forty-three-year-old (age four at the time of divorce)*

They had joint custody and we were required to spend the weekends at his house. We didn't want to and were basically forced by my dad to spend the weekends. He didn't help make the transition very easy. If anything, it made things more traumatic.

—*Twenty-four-year-old (age eight at the time of divorce)*

Unfortunately, there are no simple answers to fit all situations. The interests and needs of the children, along with the resources of both parents, need to be weighed carefully in determining the best plan. I recommend paying particular attention to the damage transplantations may cause and working to maintain nurturance and stability as the highest premium. Courts also need to take responsibility for the power and impact of court orders that place children in predicaments similar to those of the children of Darin, Mark, and Cheryl, which may create settings of emotional child abuse. It is important to be a strong advocate for your children and to provide them the opportunity to have a voice and to ultimately serve their welfare.

Nurturance for Child and Parent

The discussion of nurturance focuses on your children's needs. Meeting your children's needs so that they may experience nurturing love is dependent on the love that you have experienced. As the adage goes, "You can't give what you don't have."

This is true for all parents. If they have not been nurtured, do they really know how to provide nurturance? To love one another, we need to be loved or know love ourselves. This topic will be discussed in greater detail in chapter 9; however, as we consider the significance of nurturing our children, it is reasonable to ask, "Do we have these emotional and spiritual supplies to offer, especially if we have been recently injured or experienced crippling emotional and spiritual devastation ourselves?"

In therapy, I meet parents who were raised in intact homes, in divorced households, and in single-parent homes. They all struggle to provide quality care for their children. While their careers may be demanding, it is striking to see how many parents are more comfortable in their work environments than they are attending to their children. While parents earn points for capturing the smile and joy of that perfect family photo, that is not the whole of parenting. Parenting also includes the important and tedious details of shuttling your children to seemingly never-ending practices and encouraging them to do their schoolwork to the best of their ability. It means devoting time to your children's extracurricular activities and spending time with them, reviewing their homework, helping them practice for their plays, watching their speeches, and discovering the mystery of life itself. All this may be demanding and take away from your work at times, but the message it conveys to your children—of your investment in their lives and their self-worth—is priceless.

Divorced parents often feel depleted and unable to generate the genuine energy required for nurturing their children. If this is the case with you, you will want to attend to your own emotional and spiritual needs before you find that you are too exhausted to care for those who depend on you. When parents are replenished, they are less prone to act as Darin did, oblivious to his daughters, driven primarily by his own needs. By nurturing ourselves, we develop the stamina to manage the stormy situations described in chapter 2.

When I recognized the severity of my marital situation and the impact it had on my children, my immediate thought was to get them into individual therapy. This did not make much sense to them, as they didn't feel the need for another psychologist in their lives. When I perceived that divorce was on the horizon for my home, I recognized that my children needed independent support in addition to what I could provide.

While carefully interviewing several clinicians, I gained confidence in one particularly gifted psychologist who was recommended to work with my son. After describing the family situation and meeting with Anthony, the psychologist told me, "I'd be very happy to work with your son, but who's working with you?"

Caught off guard by his question, I quickly responded, "No one.

Focusing on myself is not where my head is at this time." He suggested that I seriously rethink what I was saying. He was right: confronting a divorce and depleting myself had consequences. I also needed help.

Of the many decisions I've made concerning my divorce, seeing a psychologist was one of the best things that I did for my family and myself. Coupled with paying attention to my physical routine (certainly among the first items to go when faced with time constraints) and making choices for healthy living, I felt more prepared to be centered and strong to care for my children. Family and friends are remarkable, but establishing a routine of necessary self-care is the first step in nurturing those around you.

Parental Recommendations

Think of the sometimes-daunting directive the flight attendant announces before a flight: in an emergency you should put your own oxygen mask on before fastening on your child's. The best way to ensure a stable, nurturing environment for your children is to put yourself in the best possible situation to care for them—and that means taking care of yourself.

1. *Pay attention to your health.* Make sure you give adequate attention to the following:
   - physical health (e.g., exercise, personal time, and proper sleep)
   - spiritual support
   - quality time with friends and relatives
   - opportunities for laughter
   - time for relaxation and play (e.g., concerts, sporting events, spa treatments, and the like)

   Many of these activities may include your children, as long as you don't feel that their presence is a drain on you—which needs to be a distinct focus. The goal is to do what strengthens and energizes you. By embracing healthy and well-rounded activities, you will serve as a role model for your children. They will feel your balance, presence, and enthusiasm, and you will set an important example for them to follow.

2. *Ask for help.* If you feel overwhelmed and incapable of parenting your children yourself, seek counseling from a professional to learn how to best respond to your children's needs. It's also okay to ask for help from trusted family and friends; however, your children still need to know that you are there for them and you continue to love them and serve as their primary guide during this critical time.

The purpose of counseling and spiritual development is to be sure that you are not burying or denying your emotions, but dealing with them instead. Over the years, I have found that divorcing parents use therapy for two reasons:

i. To deal with the crisis or stresses of divorce—managing the unexpected or overwhelming details of adjustments to this new life.

ii. To address their own selves—not in relation to their children or their spouses, but to really take a look at themselves: What are you feeling right now? How did you contribute to the estrangement? What would you do differently, if that were possible? Have you learned from this loss? How do you want to proceed with your relationships going forward?

I have found in the Divorce Study that less than 10 percent of adults experiencing divorce pursue this second kind of counseling. This is not surprising; many people who come to therapy seek relief from the *symptoms* of pain, and not the *causes* of their pain, much as in most visits for health care. Divorcing parents are less likely to examine the causes of their failed relationships or personal downfalls. They often pursue new relationships that may serve only to cover the pain or replace the emptiness of the divorce, potentially reigniting a vicious cycle. During this process, children can be left to the winds, their needs left unattended.

Our task as parents is *both* to find our optimal sources of nourishment, so that we feel empowered to manage the challenges, *and* to gain insight into ourselves on a deeper level. This provides the greatest source of peace and harmony for our homes and families.

Parents can bring balance to their lives and the home by attending to their children and to themselves—not permitting themselves to be overwhelmed, beleaguered by the challenges and tasks, or self-absorbed by attending only to their own needs. Providing nurturing for our children requires self-reflection and then assessment. Children should not be part of the fallout of divorce: they need to be assured that they remain the parents' top priority, and their goals remain the parents' goals. In chapter 5, we will consider how you can reclaim yourself to best provide for your children.

Part 2

NAVIGATING DIVORCE FOR PARENTS

Chapter 5

REGAIN CONTROL—
RECLAIM YOURSELF

I was on the verge of a mental breakdown due to my husband's constant affairs and time away from home. What the children were seeing in the way of arguments, fighting and total breakdown of a marriage was not what I wanted my children to believe a marriage should be.

—Parent (married fifteen years)

Parental Oversight 5

Divorce can be an exceptionally hard thing to accept. Yet the longer parents put off accepting it and dealing intelligently with the consequences, the longer children are exposed to potential damage. In rashly acting, re-acting, spewing information, and flailing through the intense emotional territory that is divorce, parents can lose themselves. They let the divorce define them, effectively becoming a ghost of battle rather than a whole individual. When children witness this, they lose their moorings. They view themselves as extensions of the parents; so when those parents lose themselves, the children are at sea. Your children need you to reclaim yourself, and reclaim control of the unavoidable stress of your situation, so they can continue to develop their course.

They talked *horribly* about each other. My father said, says, and will continue to say the worst things imaginable about my mom. My mom always says she never bad-mouths my dad in front of us, but she does it every time, and any time, I see her. They focused on themselves. I'm not stupid. I wasn't then and I'm not now. Although they had children, they are still children. They focus on themselves and how they were hurt and what happened to them. Through this whole thing, I *never* felt that my parents genuinely cared about what they were doing or how their actions were affecting the children.

—Twenty-year-old (age fifteen at the time of divorce)

They seemed to forget I was a human with feelings. It was all about them and what he did to her or she did to him. They acted like children and talked about each other. I used to hate that because no matter their differences, I loved them both and did not want anything bad spoken about either one.

—Forty-one-year-old (age five at the time of divorce)

My mom put all my dad's clothes and lunchbox in the car, drove to the woman he was having an affair with, and had me throw all of his clothes on the woman's lawn, knocked on the door with his lunchbox and told her to make my dad's lunch for work the next day.

—Forty-five-year-old (age twelve at the time of divorce)

Maggie, a patient of mine, could not recall a single day when her parents weren't at each other's throats. The fighting was not physical, but the intensity and abuse were no less dangerous.

Maggie mentioned that her elementary school friends would always ask why she seemed so sad. She spent most of her time at home locked in her bedroom to escape the fighting between her parents. She tried to drown out their arguments by listening to music, getting lost in a book, or shutting herself away and texting her friends.

Her parents expressed concern for her, but that did not stop them from battling with each other day and night. Maggie tried to distract them and begged them to stop, but she could not negotiate peace between them.

She hoped that once her parents divorced, her home life would settle down. Instead, even after the divorce, her parents continued to fight on the phone or whenever they saw each other in person. Constantly berating each other in her presence, her mother and father pressed Maggie to choose between them.

One of the most agonizing aspects of divorce for children is exposure to marital conflict. Children intuitively recoil when their parents are in conflict because they see themselves as extensions of their parents. Both parents are key in forming children's sense of self. Parental conflict threatens the development of a child's own identity that is separate from that of his or her parents. When there is constant conflict between parents, children feel torn. Parents' fighting leaves them feeling at odds with themselves, as if their own parents are tearing them apart.

You may recall from the discussion in chapter 2 how this draws on different parts of the brain. Our emotions—the limbic brain response (intense feelings) or the primitive brain response (the sense we are responding to matters of life and death)—prevent us from controlling these impulses. As a result, our children experience the impact of these emotional reactions, which can do real and lasting damage.

It was a constant battle for ten years. My brother and I were right smack dab in the middle. My father was always bad-mouthing my mother—calling her every derogatory name in the book. My mother, on the other hand, would never speak ill of my father. My father ended up turning my brother against our mom. I am now twenty-nine years old; my brother is almost thirty-three and he still, to this day, has hard feelings against my mother. It's still hard, even now.

—Twenty-nine-year-old (age eight at the time of divorce)

In Maggie's case, she felt there was no space for her to express her own thoughts, feelings, or opinions. She's not alone; 80 percent of children surveyed in the Divorce Study stated that they "did not express anything" regarding their feelings about the divorce. So Maggie protected herself by creating two identities—one for each parent. She went along with her mom, in support of her mom's complaints against her father; and, similarly, she affirmed her dad's complaints against her mother. Both identities were false. This is a common adaptation for children who find themselves caught in the middle of divorce warfare.

> They didn't think it impacted my life at all. Had they noticed I was devastated and stopped putting me in the middle, I would have been fine.
>
> —*Twenty-nine-year-old (age fifteen at the time of divorce)*

The sadness Maggie's friends saw in her was only the beginning of her eventual deterioration. It could have left her deeply damaged had she not sought professional help. When she came to me in high school, Maggie had disconnected from her own thoughts and feelings. Her parents' fighting had left her emotionally numb and clinically depressed, without a purpose. If her parents had regained control of themselves and the situation, Maggie could potentially take hold of herself again as well.

> They are caught in the middle, especially my older daughter who was just old enough to know something was wrong but not old enough to understand adult issues. She struggles to this day, has anxiety issues; the divorce has changed her, and, being a cautious, anxious child to begin with, transitions are really hard for her. Plus the parental alienation and involving them in adult situations and burdening them with adult issues continues to harm her and will affect her relationships for a long time to come.
>
> —*Parent (married nine years)*

STEP BACK AND RECLAIM CONTROL

Pressure and stress can get the best of us. So it's a good practice to remember to be self-observational (project yourself as someone else looking in on your interactions, and think about what you're saying and how you're acting). Don't react. Learn how to step back from the situation, breathe, and hold up a mirror to have control. How can you sail through this troubling moment? When I was fresh out of graduate school, I remember working for a very humorous publisher. Whenever things got out of control, she would engage in a full-length conversation with herself, saying things like, "I said, 'Self, what should we do with this?'" I admired her ability to distance herself from the situation and from her emotions to more ably assess what needed to be done. This mechanism gave her playful distance to avoid getting embroiled in challenging situations. A similar capacity is required if we are to accept what is happening to us and react well during the crisis of divorce.

To apply the point of regaining control and reclaiming yourself, let's review several matters that call out these capacities in order to protect our children during divorce.

ACCEPT THAT THE LEGAL PROCESS
WILL BE STRESSFUL

You will most likely experience stress because of the legal process of divorce. Even amicable divorces can be stressful, owing to the negotiations, procedures, and protocol that require protracted periods of time and energy. At the same time, your children endure stress as a result of court proceedings—even though you may be working hard to keep your children away from court matters. According to the Divorce Study, 57 percent of children felt they were brought into the middle of the legal battle, even when the divorce was not contentious or acrimonious.

> My dad stopped paying child support (for the four kids in our family), so I watched my mom struggle. She was a stay-at-home mom for the last years. Dad never called us, never wrote letters, never came to see us. He moved across the country. My mother confided in me a lot. I felt mature and I listened to her. But looking back now, I see that I was too young to deal with that much weight. As a young adult, when I wanted to reconcile with my dad, my mother was disappointed with me and said, "Oh, so after he walks out on you and has nothing to do with us for all these years, you are going to just let him waltz back in!" Those comments made it very difficult because I felt like I was betraying her.
>
> —Thirty-nine-year-old (age fifteen at the time of divorce)

During this ordeal, it is important to step back from the situation instead of reacting rashly to perceived personal affronts. Reclaim your rational brain, and observe the way you behave in front of your children. They learn from watching behavior and absorb what they see and experience, even if you are not communicating to them directly. While the court directs you not to communicate negatively about the other parent to your children and not to communicate about the legal aspects of your divorce, your children are still exposed. They cannot escape the fact that you are in the midst of handling these matters and that you manage legal issues in their presence.

It is natural for your children to feel unsure about their future. Children are hyper-attuned to the stress their parents face and are often the medium through which parents unconsciously reveal their stress, expressed by the parent's irritability, lack of patience, preoccupation, and unavailability. *A Judge's Guide: Making Child-Centered Decisions in Custody Cases*, published by the American Bar Association, is a handbook to help judges manage custody cases.[1] The following excerpt from the book describes the impact of the lengthy divorce process from a child's perspective and illustrates the distress a child feels during the court process and ruling.

A Child's Concept of Time

Imagine that you are eight years old. Your parents are divorced. You have alleged that your stepfather sexually abused you. You go to your father's home for an extended visit and report this allegation. Your father decides not to return you to your mother's custody out of concern for your safety. Through her attorney, your mother files a petition alleging visitation interference. Pending the hearing, you are allowed to remain with your father; and your mother has supervised visitation rights. The court schedules a hearing in 30 days. In addition to your case, about 30 other cases are also scheduled on the same day. The day arrives for the court hearing. Unfortunately, despite the fact that you, the parties' attorneys, and witnesses are present for the hearing, the court only hears about 30 minutes of testimony due to the crowded docket. The hearing is continued for another 30 days. The next hearing date arrives and it's yet another crowded docket. The case is once again postponed. In all, the case is tried over the course of almost two years at periodic intervals with at least three different judges presiding. Each time you appear you are reminded of your sexual encounter with your stepfather. You live with the constant fear that you will be returned to an unsafe household. Ultimately, the court decides that you should live with your father permanently.

Unfortunately, the above scenario is based on a true case and not uncommon. A lack of expedited decision-making in child custody cases hurts children.

As we've discussed in Maggie's story, children feel silenced during the divorce process; they are not often permitted information that affects their family, home, or parents. As a result, there is plenty of opportunity for children to imagine and internalize fearful outcomes.

This is compounded when parents don't react well to the stresses of the legal process; instead, parents who are caught up in a hostile divorce frequently become focused on winning the battle or defeating their spouses. Instead of speaking with a voice of reason, we can function irrationally, with emotional reactivity (primarily from the limbic brain). Or we can function aggressively, as if battling to save ourselves from harm (primarily from the primitive brain). **When these battles take center stage—regardless of whether or not you win—your children lose.** As difficult as it may be to manage the actions of your spouse, you will realize when functioning rationally (using your neocortex) that your primary focus should demonstrate your efforts to preserve and nurture the emotional and physical health of your children. Then you can ensure you are appropriately focused and connected to their needs and development.

When you act in your children's best interests using your neocortex brain, rather than reacting with the primal limbic and primitive brains, you will be less likely to endanger your children by putting them in the middle of a war zone. This is the goal. In some instances, the spouse may be out of control. In these situations, with the support of appropriate professionals, you will be supported in your management of the divorce and your interventions on your children's behalf.

> My father caught my mother making love with someone else. They went to court and my father had my mother accused of being a bad mother. My father didn't want custody; he just did not want my mother to get it. My maternal grandparents took custody. They raised me until I was thirteen years old. Then I went to live with my mother. As a result, I still wrestle with feelings of insecurity, low self-esteem, and poor self-image.
>
> —*Fifty-seven-year-old (age three at the time of divorce)*

Accept That You Must Communicate with Your Ex-Spouse

Parents going through a divorce tend to judge situations in black and white—all or nothing, like normal small children. Several judges have shared with me how they anticipate what parents in a contentious divorce will say during the court proceedings because of their charged emotionality. Judges have told me that frequently such parents predictably level charges of a psychological disorder against the other parent. Outbursts that claim, "She's bipolar!" or "He's a narcissist!" are not uncommon. While such charges may muddy the waters, judges are trained to attend to violations and proven facts over ambiguous charges, particularly those violations against the children.

It's not easy to keep peace and maintain presence of mind when tensions are high or when you feel emotionally or physically in danger. Consider Maggie and how her parents' behavior led to her shutting down. She became emotionally unavailable. The stress at home drove her to disconnect her thoughts from her feelings, affecting her identity and placing her at risk to experience serious negative consequences. While parents are fighting for their children, the *manner* in which they fight for them can easily destroy their children's well-being.

Like Maggie, children often struggle to choose a side or attempt to negotiate peace settlements between their parents. Battling parents want to remember that no matter who is right or who is wrong, the children require protection through active attentiveness.

> I was robbed of a childhood. So, no, I don't know what it's like to be a kid because I never got the chance to be.
> —Eighteen-year-old *(age seventeen months at the time of divorce)*

During a divorce, it is common for one parent to hold the polar opposite viewpoint from the other parent, which displays the effort to distance oneself. While it may be reasonable to differ, parents who find it impossible to maintain civility in their children's presence should agree to communicate away from the children, for example, via e-mail or text messages. Electronic communication, or other indirect means for exchanges, can buffer the intensity of the situation and provide time to reread messages before sending them. Alternatively, in emotionally charged situations, parents should consider communicating through professionals, such as their lawyers, to avoid subjecting children to warfare and hostility.

What Are Your Actions Saying?

Maggie, like many children of divorce, experienced role reversal; she was like a mother struggling to manage her children with behavioral problems. For example, consider these lines:

> Her parents expressed concern for her, but that did not stop them from battling day and night. She tried to distract them and begged them to stop, but she could not negotiate peace between them.

Replacing the word *parents* with *children* clearly demonstrates the picture. Maggie's parents were behaving like petulant children—exactly the way the parents taught her not to act!

When parents examine their responses, they often find—as most of us do after we react emotionally—that they have reenacted relationships from their earlier struggles, possibly as a result of problematic dynamics they observed in their own homes. Their acting-out behavior appears to be on autopilot, resurfacing during a divorce and following intense situations. Endeavors to understand the underpinnings of divorce usually reveal patterns of distress. When counseling divorced parents, it is common to uncover unresolved issues from childhood that remained unaddressed—issues that later took a toll on their marriage.

> I was very promiscuous and had almost no self-esteem. I repeated the cycle of divorce with my own children. I went through four marriages before I finally sought therapy. I found out that my parents' divorce and the subsequent abuse by my mother had scarred me very badly. I am grateful for the help that I received and only wish I had gone for help sooner. I am now a 4.0 student majoring in psychology. I am fifty-six.
>
> —*Fifty-six-year-old (age six at the time of divorce)*

I've never been able to trust males in my life. My mom married three times and was engaged a fourth time. None of those men were able to be a dad or a father to me. I am still single perhaps because I quickly sabotage any relationship I have with males in my life.

—*Forty-six-year-old (age five at the time of divorce)*

Certainly, ending a relationship and starting anew with the same unresolved problems sounds like a repeated cycle of disappointment. Statistics confirm that second marriages have a higher probability of failure than first marriages—around 66 percent; and third marriages around 75 percent.[2] Problems underlying character and emotional issues that affected the first marriage will typically reoccur and impose similar relational difficulties on subsequent relationships—unless they are corrected. As a result, parents undergoing divorce may not only act like children, but they may also act like the children they once were, owing to unresolved childhood issues. The black-and-white, all-or-nothing, "the other spouse is all wrong and I am all right" perception is a pattern of thinking attributed to young children who understand life in less-complex ways.

To avoid the pitfalls of this process, listen carefully to what those around you are saying—that is, not only venting your understandable challenges but paying attention to how your reactions are received by your children, friends, and others. Certainly, if you're feeling intense emotional reactions, seeking a professional sounding board (through counseling and spiritual guidance) can provide an avenue for safe, more objective reflection on your management.

ACCEPT DIVORCE WITHOUT NORMALIZING

When attempting to accept the reality of a divorce, a common reaction is to normalize divorce wholesale, and use its "normalcy" to put off working through the trauma. Some researchers support this attitude by claiming that children of divorce generally only experience "short-term negative consequences of divorce." They report that the majority of divorced children do not exhibit distinguishable long-term consequences when compared to children of intact families.[3] Both claims are unsubstantiated by the Divorce Study and are counterintuitive and contrary to most understanding of developmental psychology, which is explained further in chapter 7. The Divorce Study affirms the conclusion that children exposed to high levels of marital discord do better *following* divorce when compared to children who endure ongoing parental distress. Less than one quarter (21 percent) of children welcomed divorce as a reprieve from their parents' marriage and were pleased to hear of their parents' divorce. Yet divorce meant that these children were removed from toxic situations more quickly, therefore enduring less suffering and receiving the opportunity for more nurturance from their parents.

Divorce is more prevalent in modern times, resulting in less social stigma than in previous decades.[4] Yet the effort to normalize divorce as not significantly problematic was *not* the experience of children participating in the Divorce Study. Studies about the effects of divorce often draw distinctly different conclusions because there are many intervening variables and each divorce is different. There is a tendency to label families and sanitize the effects. For instance, homes are labeled as modern variations of the family—as "blended families" or "single-parent homes."

Rather than recognizing the disorganization and negative impacts divorce has on children, people may dismiss them as if they were simply modern sociological adaptations of the family. The results from the Divorce Study and my personal and professional experience lead me to conclude that the antidote to adverse consequences of divorce is found in the parents' ability and children's capacity to bond, process, and work through the distress and potential trauma; it is not simply to accept and normalize divorce as a typical hurdle, without consequences for the child or society.

I have little empathy for two adults who just "part ways" after creating a life, because that life will forever pay for or live out the consequences of the mistakes of the two who created it.

—Twenty-seven-year-old (age two at the time of divorce)

ACCEPT THE REASONS YOU DIVORCED

By understanding yourself and taking control of your parenting, you resolve to get off the runaway train that can lead you, your children, and your family off course. You reclaim yourself when you assess the functionality of your family life, take a personal inventory of your relationships, and identify whether you and your family are living a meaningful life. A key part of this is understanding and accepting what has happened to your marriage. The marriage relationship accesses your neocortex's vision, your limbic system's emotional embrace, and your reptilian brain's basic needs from security to sex. Ideally, in a marriage, you want to identify if your brain is functioning fully in the course of daily life with your spouse.

When this isn't the case, the marriage hasn't necessarily failed—you wouldn't want to assign a death certificate even in the face of a catastrophic illness. Jumping to conclusions is unhelpful and a product of reactivity. However, if a marriage is off track, one can presume that the children are not enjoying an optimal setting in which to develop—and you really can't have a marriage unless both spouses are in it.

Most marriages begin without each partner having a complete understanding of one's self or one's spouse. While they have idealistic hopes, dreams, and visions of how the relationship will evolve, they rarely make a clear inventory of the resources available or develop a substantial understanding of the other person. Your future is impossible to know, and most of us realize that we don't fully know ourselves, much less another person. Quite frequently in marriage counseling, I find people who feel driven to push a square peg into a round hole. In other words, people often expect that the other person *is* or will *be* what they had in mind, rather than recognizing the other person for who he or she is. In the face of anticipation, we gloss over details that don't fit our schema, or we excuse problems or deny red flags. Later, we find that we have to deal with what exists and may have to abandon our expectations of what we thought the relationship was. A genuine marriage commitment works by acknowledging the unanticipated and unexpected events together, while working toward a negotiation regarding unperceived and undesirable qualities.

Additionally, in marriage we recognize that automatic, unresolved behaviors and patterns from our own childhoods, as previously referenced, may be factors blocking the effective flow for communication. The so-called baggage of the other person that all spouses inherit in a marriage may become an unalterable issue. We have the responsibility to recognize what we bring into our relationships, and to identify the accommodation we need for our idiosyncrasies. Only then will a marriage commitment enable us to resolve undesirable aspects and grow together.

Therefore, you don't have to react to irrational actions in your relationship—you don't have to be *that* person—because being *that* person does not serve you. If you fail to effectively confront the inherited features of your marriage, you may find yourself stuck and feel as though you're banging your head against the wall, realizing that complaining will not change your concerns or make your dream come true.

So far, we have considered the management of typical divorce situations that run the gamut from contested to controversial. Yet there are a number of marital situations that general directives do not cover. These occur when your spouse is compromised emotionally, functioning dangerously, or placing you and your children at risk. So far, we have focused on situations wherein parents are entitled to equal rights. However, contrary to the claims of anger by both parties, sometimes accusations of narcissism, sociopathic behavior, or bipolar disorder are, in fact, realities. When this is the case, the stakes become much more complex and severe for you and your children.

SANDY'S STORY

Sandy's case tested my skills and stumped my efforts at time-tested guidance. Over the years, I have witnessed many families who have endured abusive marriages and unfair divorce rulings for various reasons: they did not want to break up the family, they feared insecurity, or they lacked resources. Sandy's story relates a parent's special need to gain control of one's self and protect one's children during an extreme case of physical abuse following divorce:

> My divorce finalized joint parental rights and shared parenting time. My ex had visitations every other weekend and an order for child support. I signed the decree. This was my hope that it would bring an end to the control and abuse by my ex-husband. Unfortunately, it was neither upheld by my ex nor enforced by the courts.
>
> I am greatly concerned for the safety of my children under their father's care. The rights of my children are not honored or respected by their father! When my children return from visits with him, there are often signs of abuse—both emotional and sometimes physical. A few summers ago, my ex, who now lives out of my state, had his two-week visitation with the children and kept them for five weeks. He and his wife were screening all contact with my children and refused to return my children to me. Despite many hours of seeking help, nothing was done to enforce his contempt of court. When the children were finally returned to my care, my ten-year-old son Josh sat on my lap and wept hysterically, begging me not to send him back to his father because he was afraid of him. While he sat there in my arms, crying, he peed his pants.
>
> I have made numerous reports and taken pictures of the physical abuse of my children, but these have not led to any legal action. Similar to other cases of abuse and neglect, the investigator asks the abuser about the incidents. With the children running the risk of more abuse for talking about it, they are afraid to speak. I am

at a point where I refuse to report anything because my children no longer speak about what happens due to the fear of further repercussions. The children will no longer openly talk to their counselors, teachers, or friends, and when my children do talk to me, they beg me not to tell anyone.

One of the hardest experiences for me is when my children return from their five-week overstayed visit with their father; and I have to send them back once again for another. I have to look my children in the eye and tell them that they have to go, even though they continuously cry.

Such was the last time I would see my son Josh alive. During that visit my ex was reportedly playing video games as he gave our son Josh permission to ride an adult four-wheeler. Josh went for a ride without any supervision or proper gear and lost control, causing him to run into a barbwire fence. He was later found dead by his sister. The time span from the crash to locating Josh is not known. The father and stepmother then made arrangements for a burial without my knowledge or consent. When I learned about the incident, I made quick arrangements to get to my children and Josh's body. However, I was not able to see Josh until he was brought back home, a few days after his death. At that point, my ex took me to court immediately to lower his child support even though he had not paid for two years.

I am tired of fighting for justice when my voice is not heard! My children are afraid of their father and ask me to help them; yet no matter where I turn I get sent to someone else, as my ex knows how to play the system. I have written many letters to media and have put my children in counseling. I am greatly concerned that another incident may happen! My son is dead because of their father's negligence. Despite reports made, nothing or no one has changed this continuously threatening situation. Why must my children be forced to spend time with an adult who only brings them distress and fear?

I can prove my case with recordings, numerous e-mails from my ex, with pictures and witnesses. I am even willing to get evaluated. I have absolutely nothing to hide. I want my children to be heard, to be safe, and to not fear for their lives! I greatly regret that not one person has been willing to defend them. My children have lost everything and their brother, Josh, whom I couldn't keep safe. I believe the freedom that is meant to defend my children has instead become the freedom that allows this man to continue neglecting and abusing our children.

Sandy was not in a position to control the behavior of her ex-husband. She stated that she was doing everything in her power to protect her children and that she and her children remained helpless. Hostility between parents was dramatic in Sandy's relationship with her ex-spouse and turned abusive with the children who were caught in the middle.

Studies universally agree that whenever a child witnesses the ongoing parental anguish and fighting as a result of divorce, it is among the most disturbing experiences for kids.[5] Sometimes children cannot be shielded from their parents' poor actions.

These issues become even more extreme in cases like Sandy's when children become the objects of dangerous parental actions, as expressed by other contributors to the Divorce Study.

My father made Oregon news by fighting and winning custody of his five sons. His lawyer discovered my mother had fled to Nevada for a quickie divorce, and lied to officials about her residency. They threatened her with the law if she did not do entirely what our father asked. He lied to my mom about having a vasectomy after doctors told her another pregnancy would be dangerous. She became pregnant with another boy who basically became the final straw [before the divorce]. My youngest brother knew he was the reason our parents separated; he committed suicide in his twenties.

—*Sixty-year-old (age sixteen at the time of divorce)*

ACCEPT THE REALITY OF INJUSTICE

In Massachusetts, I serve as a guardian ad litem (GAL), which is a professional psychologist or attorney appointed by the court to report on and advise on matters regarding minors or people who need special protection from the court (such as elderly or incompetent individuals). Judges have disclosed to me the painful and complex decision-making process that goes into rendering "just" custody decisions. Indeed, courts can also make poor decisions and hold judges unaccountable for custody rulings that hurt children. Kathleen Russell, founding executive director for the Center for Judicial Excellence; Connie Valentine, cofounder of the California Protective Parents Association; and I have been collaborating to bring attention to public child abuse resulting from poor custody decisions.

In a televised show with Dr. Phil, Kathleen revealed the disturbing fact that attorneys in California often guide their clients *not* to report child abuse, lest *they* lose custody completely. The reasoning behind this is that the court system is so overwhelmed and motivated by expediency and self-serving interests that judges often automatically consider such claims nefarious and remove custody from the parent who reports the abuse. Adding insult to literal injury, these judges may place the child in the custody of the abusive parent.

> I would like to hear more about breaking the cycle of abuse. People still don't want to talk about it. Families don't want to get involved. If they do get involved, they don't know or understand how they are enabling the abuser by making one excuse after the next, therefore, not holding the abuser accountable for his actions.
>
> —*Parent (married five years)*

While it should be comforting to know that the legal system will prevail with just determinations, this is not always the case. If you are facing a potentially dangerous situation with your ex-spouse, it is essential to lead in this process with your most sophisticated brain. Nevertheless, you may find yourself alone at times, like Sandy, and that the road to justice is demanding and elusive. Until there are significant reforms in the legal system and those in positions of evaluation and judgments are held accountable, abused children will not necessarily remain safe in divorce courts. There continues to be a need for standardization in the process for custody reports by court evaluators and recourse for extreme cases.

> I believe that instead of making things better in divorce, the family courts have made things more adversarial. I get it: to dissolve a marriage and protect yourself legally/financially you have to go to court. But this is a no-win situation. You cannot split up families fairly, so what ends up happening is compromise and everyone gets less than the best, and everyone "loses."
>
> —*Seventeen-year-old (age fourteen at the time of divorce)*

It's understandable if you feel out of control and beside yourself when court rulings do not confirm your truth. Appealing sounds like the rational alternative, but sometimes the court action, the costs, or the lack of emotional resources leave you too overwhelmed and disabled to press on. You may feel unfairly judged and that you have been ripped off, marginalized, or vilified. Now is the time for resetting yourself, centering, and reclaiming your priorities. You may find that taking a spiritual perspective is critical for healing. While licking your wounds, asking for sympathy, and giving in to tears are totally appropriate, you want to do the following:

- Reclaim your vision—what you believe both about the big questions of life and about what needs to happen to best support your children.
- Understand what transpired.
- Differentiate between rational thoughts and emotional feelings, and make sure each is attended to.

- Establish an effective plan for proceeding.
- Use opportunities available for you to re-present your intentions and truth.
- Own your errors.
- Recognize your strengths.
- Work to make the best situation of what is available to you.
- Consider alternative strategies for going forward.

Parental Recommendations

Because the divorce process is such a stressful experience in life, give yourself distance and respond appropriately so that you best serve yourself and your children. Consider these three key truths to reclaim yourself:

- *Accept that divorce has painful consequences.* Recognize that this is one of the most stressful challenges you will face with your children and family. You will regularly be thrown curveballs, and you'll need to be on your toes, with your head in the game. This means not abandoning your responsibilities or allowing some of these responsibilities to fall onto your children's laps. When the unexpected occurs—and it will—correct it and move forward.
- *Recognize that your ex-spouse is no longer your spouse.* Though you may still co-parent, you may suffer from communication difficulties. These difficulties may even have resulted in your breakup. At a minimum, your ex-spouse thinks differently than you do and is entitled to do so. One of the greatest problems we struggle with in communication, especially in marital situations—and even furthermore in divorce—is *differentiation* or recognizing that each person thinks differently. In chapter 2, we discussed how our brains are not simply driven by rational judgment but by visceral drives. Additionally, while we know that we are individuals with unique personalities, we often forget

and *project*, which means that we think the other person will respond as we think he or she needs to respond. In this way, we fail to *differentiate*. In response, we may not be understanding but rather judgmental, critical, and angry. Rather than simply reacting to your ex-spouse, it may be helpful to try to see his or her behavior from your spouse's point of view—to determine how he or she thinks *differently* (in a way that's not inherently wrong) than the way you think. This does not suggest that you agree with that thought process. But it may allow you to have a different perspective and help you resolve issues before they turn into disagreements. This will also spare your child the pain of being put in the middle of contentious parenting exchanges. Of course, this is not to imply that you should change your perspective— simply that you should respectfully recognize that there are differences.

- *Keep your identity intact.* The publisher I mentioned earlier playfully demonstrated an important tactic for finding oneself— not just acting and reacting in life but seeking to be in touch with who she was—by engaging her observational self or talking with herself. For many people, the first time they come to therapy is when they are dealing with a crisis. However, many parents recognize that therapy is also a useful tool of self-care that assists them with their childcare during divorce. Recognize that you are more than your actions and reactions. You are a person with an identity, and you may lose sight of your own person as you become part of this contentious situation in your life. If you lose yourself, as Maggie's parents did, you may also potentially lose your child.

The courts are not perfect. Custody evaluators have turned over children to parental predators and abusers because of inaccurate assessments and the courts' formulaic posture of entitled shared custody for parents. In such situations, courts can re-traumatize victims of abuse and blame good, decent, and protective parents for trying to shield their children from verifiably abusive parents.

If you think that you have been treated unfairly in your court proceedings, you may feel as though you're engaged in yet another battle or a battle you cannot win. Your drive, fortitude, and stamina can guide you to persevere until your legal issues are resolved. You do not need to react but, instead, must act appropriately in such encounters with your spouse and your children to bring forward your truth and the best results.

Most people do not consider divorce to be an opportunity for change, but like most challenges we face in life, it can create an opportunity for significant growth. If you pursue therapy in the throes of divorce, you are entitled to your therapist's empathic ear. However, see this as an opportunity to assess both *yourself* and your situation. It won't be possible to learn the lessons of divorce if you only address the emotional tailspin. For the benefit of yourself and your children, therapy is an opportune time to explore your role, choices, actions, and personal baggage. Use this opportunity to gain control of yourself and your parenting and to reclaim your life and family. If your therapist is not helping you in this process, find a new one. Therapists are understandably not effective with every client, and finding the right one for you is paramount.

In the introduction to this book, I mentioned that a humbling 67 percent of children who underwent professional therapy during their parents' divorce said the therapy was "unhelpful" or "a waste of time." These are disturbing statistics about the effectiveness of clinicians. These numbers do not mean that the therapists were not empathetic or insightful, but they were unsuccessful in leading their patients to a clearer understanding. That doesn't have to be the same for you. Not only do you need someone to hear you in therapy, but you also need a professional who helps you build awareness of your situation and the significance of your decisions and actions for both your life and your child's life. The stakes are very high. In addition to your individual work, it may be possible to seek counseling with your ex-spouse while co-parenting so that you can learn how to best manage your new roles. Though you may feel provoked by the multiple stressors affecting you simultaneously, it's valuable to remain focused on the real prize: your children and their needs. Support is key to making the best choices.

Chapter 6 will guide you in your efforts toward creating meaningful relationships and healing the fractured trust that has affected your children.

Chapter 6

REALIGN YOUR RELATIONSHIPS

[They] kept telling me they knew how I felt, even though they'd never gone through it. Then when they would tell me what they thought I was feeling, it wasn't right. When I would tell them how I felt, they would tell me I was wrong.

—Forty-seven-year-old (age twelve at the time of divorce)

Parental Oversight 6

You may move on after a divorce and expect your children to do the same. You want to keep in mind, however, that many children develop a misguided sense of trust and intimacy that, unless addressed, can have long-term effects on their ability to trust and form loving relationships as adults.

> I find it extremely difficult to trust. I sometimes think that I wasn't loved, or shown love, or taught how to love and deal with relation- ships. I feel like no one will ever love me. I've tried to love and give my all. The problem is I made really bad choices in whom I chose. As the saying goes: my picker's broke; so I stopped picking.
> —*Fifty-four-year-old (age fourteen at the time of divorce)*

They did nothing. They never talked to us about how it made us feel or why. They just went on with their lives, like they were kids again who didn't have any responsibilities. It really did hurt to feel like you were no longer a kid with a parent at the age of twelve. I just felt like an individual who was just thrown into the world's uncertainties with no warning.

—*Seventeen-year-old (age eleven at the time of divorce)*

I hate that I don't feel as if I can relax in life and be trusting. I feel "weird." I feel as if I'm always being judged. I just miss the confidence that I had until my parents divorced. I don't feel worthy anymore. I'm definitely a "self-abuser," and I hate it!

—*Twenty-seven-year-old (age three at the time of divorce)*

Megan was in eighth grade when she came to family therapy. Her parents had divorced a few years earlier, and she and her siblings lived with their father. Megan did not present herself with any particular concerns and maintained solid academic, athletic, and social engagements in her young life. As a result, the idea of family therapy seemed unnecessary to her. Nonetheless, her father thought it might be potentially helpful for the family to attend counseling to review the changes that had transpired. Following the divorce, Megan's mom had started a new relationship and gained a new family in her husband's children, but her mom did not seem to understand that her actions affected her own children. On the whole, the family reported that Megan's mother was removed from their family life, and the children had no interest in maintaining contact with their mother at that time. As part of the interviewing process, I met with the family members individually.

I often invite patients to share with me examples of music they've played or sung, essays or poetry they've written, or art they've created. These creative constructions often provide vehicles to engage conversations that reveal their inner thoughts and feelings more vividly than words alone.

While the children in Megan's family spoke openly during family sessions about the divorce and owned their critical feelings about their mom, they also conveyed their belief that they had worked through these issues previously and felt comfortable functioning freely—without obstacles—as they pursued their life goals and activities.

Megan said that she had put the divorce behind her but then recalled and shared the following poem that she had written for English class—one year following the divorce:

When the Sidewalk Ends

Loving her,
Is the way I cared for her.
Through opening my heart,
I shared my soul.

But then she takes advantage of my love,
She lies straight to my face.
All the joys we've shared together,
All of the summers we spent together,
Were those all lies; was she just deceiving me?

I feel like a stranger is sitting before me,
Having shared my secrets,
All of my special moments with this person,
Did she care about me?
Or was she just using me?

I've tried to understand what has happened,
But remain in a tailspin with no understanding.
That person wants to move on,
Venture into a new life,
But getting left like dirt from the bottom of her shoe,
I am discarded.

Pictures on the wall feign joy;
Memories sleep in photo albums,
But those pictures, and those memories,
Lack the spark of authenticity.

Many days have passed.
The walk is coming to an end.

Short lived.
The sidewalk ends.
As for that person, the one I felt I could trust,
The one who would be there for my every step;
She has left me, and I have to move on.

People take action not knowing the consequences.
Know with whom you share your soul,
So that you're not left alone.
Don't be fooled by people
Lest the sidewalk ends.

Consider these questions after reading Megan's poem:

- What do you think Megan is saying?
- If she were your child, how would you respond to what she wrote?
- Do you think Megan truly put the divorce behind her?

When I asked Megan about her relationship with her mom, she responded nonchalantly, "My mom has not been part of my life. I've had great friends and have a lot of support from my dad and family members. At this point, it's really not much different than losing a best friend who moved away long ago. It's sad; and I expressed that. But I adjusted. I have moved on and count this as a loss. I have no plans to waste more time to meet her needs to preserve the idea that she has been my mom, because she really wasn't there for me."

I shared with Megan my belief that she had worked through a great deal and had made some strong decisions. I was impressed with Megan—by her articulate grasp of her feelings and that she had not felt derailed in her own path because of her parents' divorce. As discussed in chapter 3, many children are emotionally impaired and "parentified" when their roles are reversed with their parents'. Children are suddenly made to act like grownups, caring for their own parents' needs. Megan clearly felt that she had spent a great deal of time coming to terms with her parents' divorce and that she was happy and fully engaged with her life. She explained how she did not want to lose any more time trying to relive lost moments—as a lot of time and counseling had been directed at that—or to respond to her mom who may now want to attend to her, recognizing a need for Megan in her life.

Despite Megan's incisive and decisive position and sense that this was behind her, I told her that I could still feel her strong pulse, a throbbing heartache in her poems, that conveyed emotional pain.

Megan answered, "Of course, I have feelings about these events. This is not a poem that ends, 'And they lived happily ever after.' This was also an assignment for class, and I tried to resurface the drama." She smiled. "But I don't think that I'm kidding myself. Divorce made me grow up fast, and I'm happy that I had and have the support that I need to move on with my life."

It can be difficult for children to accept the choices their parents make during a divorce. Even when children appear to have adjusted or resolved their relationships with their parents—as with Megan and her mother—there may be substantial work to be done in order to repair damaged trust.

Megan's poems communicate feelings that she may not recognize or doesn't feel prepared to address. At this point, however, she was not seeking to reopen this relationship. In general, **you cannot tell children**

what they are feeling or impose on them feelings they are not ready to address. Children are likely to talk about their thoughts when they feel safe, comfortable, and ready. They also must know that you care and that their feelings matter. You build this atmosphere of trust by talking *with* your children rather than at them.

Likewise, the courts cannot effectively make children want to participate in parenting reunification programs and visitations against the child's will (though they formally and legally issue such orders and visitation rules that the court will enforce). Megan reported that she had heard there was a court effort to order a reunification program; she adamantly stated that she would not want to waste time in such unpleasant and distressing meetings. While reunification efforts and visitations can improve broken relationships between children and parents, it's important to assess whether an individual child is ready for such efforts.

I don't believe there are hard and fast rules to determine when and how your children will talk about their feelings. It is true, however, that you are less likely to get cooperation with your children—particularly adolescents—when you pressure them to reveal feelings against their will. Their cooperation is contingent on their readiness, comfort, understanding, and feeling of safety with you. In the face of a ruptured relationship, the goal is to give them opportunities to share their feelings with you and show them they can depend on your sensitivity and constructive actions in their lives.

> My father was definitely the most helpful during the divorce because he was always there for me; and I just felt like he wanted me more than my mom.
>
> —*Fifteen-year-old (age seven at the time of divorce)*

> The night before Dad left, he told me that he was going away for a while to become a better person, but that he would be back.

He asked me how I felt about it. At that time, I thought he was serious; and I supported that idea. I thought if he left for a little while with the result of coming back a better person that was an admirable thing to do. So I said "okay." The very next day, when he left without even saying goodbye, I knew he was not really coming back; and I wished that I had not given him my consent.

—*Thirty-nine-year-old (age fifteen at the time of divorce)*

It can be difficult for children to accept the choices their parents make during a divorce. Even when children appear to have adjusted or resolved their relationships with their parents—as with Megan and her mother—there may be substantial work to be done. As previously stated, parents and the courts cannot effectively impose these actions on children—particularly when they are adolescents and have strong feelings. A child's feelings and acts of expression evolve through his or her own psychological readiness during the divorce process. Children are in dire need of support from parents who are invested in their feelings, and who talk *with* them rather than *at* them. Parents are not usually effective in healing ruptures in their relationships with their children when they interpret, scold, criticize, or force the child or the other parent. **Talking *at* your children does not work. Talking *with* your children leads to constructive growth.**

TRUST IN YOUR RELATIONSHIP WITH YOUR CHILD

You may not make every meet, practice, or game, or even attend every Parents' Night at your kids' school, but that is not the measure of a healthy relationship. Psychologists often say that healthy relationships can be measured by the quality and ease of connecting, disconnecting, and reconnecting; of engagement, disengagement, and re-engagement;

of coming together and moving apart. If you have a solid bond with your children, your physical absence will not always be detrimental because trust is solid in its emotional core. Your children do not need you to be tied at their hip to know you love them. You can engage and disengage fluidly and naturally, recognizing that you are both separate yet connected; you are interdependent. Thus, there needs to be space for individual choices that accommodate each family member's personal time and engagement. I recall my university professor of personality psychology emphasizing that quality of time is what makes the difference in "good" parenting—parenting that is philosophically, spiritually, and psychologically sound. My observation from my clinical work and personal life is that both *quality* and *quantity* of time are essential.

> Perhaps my dad would have been emotionally distant in the home if he had stayed, but as a result of the conditions of my parents' divorce, I never married. I have no trouble attracting men; but I don't keep them. I often feel lost and have a strong sense of not belonging even though I have family nearby and a history with many of the people in my life. I've realized the effects the lack of fathering has had on me; but that may be less about the divorce and more about the abandonment.
>
> *—Thirty-seven-year-old (age six at the time of divorce)*

Secretive and disconnected engagements that are deceitful or that shut members out of the family are best avoided; these actions do not respect the dignity of all involved. More fundamentally, such behaviors counter the definition of family and establish the basis for a breakdown of the relationships between family members. These situations confirm that we cannot have our cake and eat it too. As Megan's mother sought to recapture missed experiences with her children years after the divorce, the obstacles she encountered required her to accept the consequences of her earlier disconnection.

SOPHIA'S STORY

When Tina came to see me, she was shaken up and in despair after her eldest daughter, Sophia, discovered that her father, Marcus, was texting and chatting online with a woman about their romantic rendezvous.

Marcus, a globe-trotting businessman, and Tina, a stay-at-home mom, had been married for twenty-one years. The couple had three children, ages twelve, fourteen, and sixteen. Marcus was a strict disciplinarian who maintained a rather distant, traditional role within his family. Tina managed the family's daily activities and served as the emotional and spiritual center of the home.

While she had been aware of her husband's affairs, Tina had put up with his infidelity to keep the family intact. She was surprised, however, when Marcus announced that he wanted a divorce. Sophia was not surprised.

The parenting challenge that Marcus faced was expecting and demanding that his children trust in his love for them, even as he engaged in inappropriate behaviors that seriously confused and angered them, which confirmed for them that he was not trustworthy. It was a clear case of actions speaking louder than words.

Sophia became outraged and disgusted with her father's behavior. She rebelled when he announced that he wanted to share custody with their mother. She lashed out by exposing to her father all the e-mails that she had gathered as evidence of his affairs. Marcus was stunned that his beloved daughter had exposed him, but he was self-deceived by thinking that she would continue to love and obey him even when he betrayed her trust.

For children, the breakup of a family can serve as a premature wake-up call to the uncertainty of life. Divorce often destroys children's trusted image of their parents, and it throws the parent-child relationship out of balance. Kids end up reassessing what is real, whom they can trust, and what they need to feel secure. If parents are not available to help them make sense of these situations—as in Marcus's case—children learn not to trust their parents. They'll begin to see relationships as fleeting and undependable, and they often question their own worth. In these situations, children learn fear and uncertainty rather than trust.

RETAINING TRUST WITH CHILDREN OF DIVORCE

The powerful experience of *trust* serves as a cornerstone and is pivotal for healthy development. Children seek opportunities for exploration and rely on a secure foundation, provided by their parents, to explore the fascinating possibilities of life. But children often find that this experience comes to a screeching halt in the face of their parents' divorce. Simply put, divorce often puts trust in jeopardy.

> They went on with their lives and were happy and didn't seem to give a thought to how it was affecting me and my sisters. From that time on I always promised myself I would take care of myself.
> —*Forty-four-year-old (age seven at the time of divorce)*

If you felt as though you were on trial when you were in court, imagine how your children felt. As described in chapter 5, parents in a divorce need to remember that their children are highly attuned to threatening behaviors. Therefore, children sometimes react to their parents in a variety of stress-inducing ways because their trust has been challenged. Divorcing parents often feel as if their children are scrutinizing them—and for good reason. Parents understandably seek to regain their children's trust both in their relationships with them now and in the value of relationships going forward.

In this chapter, we have considered the claims of Megan and Sophia, who felt emotionally violated by the actions of their mother and father, respectively. It would not be surprising if these girls' parents, who had been rejected by their children, also claimed that their daughters were alienated or brainwashed by their respective spouses.

Alienation and Brainwashing

Two words commonly used in courts during child custody arguments are *alienation* and *brainwashing*. *Parental alienation syndrome* is a theory asserting that a parent may "bad-mouth" or brainwash a child to turn him or her against the other parent. This is often done by who wants more custody, who wants to limit the other parent's access to the child, or who wants to enact revenge. The alienation theory is highly controversial—and several professionals have discredited it as "bad science" because it is often used as an explanation for why children do not respond to a parent when the truth is the parent's own actions have caused the estrangement.[1] At the same time, there is no question that it has been taken seriously in courts, as it is also true that parents can influence children's perception and understanding of the situation, particularly when children are put in the middle of the divorce.

One parent in the Divorce Study stated:

> People need to become aware of the theory called "Parental Alienation Syndrome." That's when the primary parent does all they can to turn the child against the "targeted" parent through things like lies, skipping visits, manipulating the child's mind, etc. It does more than brainwash them. It programs their mind to be against the other parent who has tried to be there for them, but who isn't allowed to be there. The targeted parent is bullied on a regular basis; but the courts do nothing to help them! It eventually gets to where the child doesn't even know what the truth is anymore!
>
> —*Parent (married twenty-two years)*

I believe that each divorce case must be assessed on its own merits. While I am not convinced that, in general, a parent claiming parental alienation accurately describes the dynamics leading to a child's mistrust, I believe that children are attracted to the parent who more clearly meets their needs and can be influenced to alienate a parent. Children do not necessarily discriminate between the parent's motives and their reasons for seeking custody or claiming alienation. I think it is imperative for parents to ask themselves whether their motives are in the best interest of the children, yet I know that getting emotional parents to think rationally is not an easy order as they, too, are frightened, angry, and not necessarily thinking clearly.

The following questions may help you examine your motives and behavior concerning both custody and alienation:

- Are you present for your child?
- What are the real reasons you seek custody?
- Do you believe you can best facilitate your child's growth or that your ex-spouse may impose damage?
- Is this just about getting revenge against your ex-spouse by winning the legal battle?
- Do you seek to remove the other person from your life and the lives of your children?
- To what extent on a scale of zero to ten (zero meaning not at all and ten meaning completely) do your needs or those of your children drive your motives?

One of my patients shared with me how she had dismissed her father for years on the basis of the attitudes she had adopted from her mother, whom she identified with at the time of her parents' divorce. The father was viewed as a "monster" and "irresponsible," and she kept him at a distance—which was easy because her mother held full physical and legal custody, regularly cautioning her daughter about the father's wily behavior. When my patient married and the couple engaged in cordial exchanges with her parents, the patient's husband helped her recognize that her father was actually quite reasonable. In fact, it was her mother who had demonstrated manipulative and controlling behaviors, and had been "villainizing" the patient's dad for years. My patient recognized that she never gave her dad a chance, and that he retained distance out of respect and in an effort not to provoke her mother, who reacted very harshly. While her father tried and could possibly have made stronger overtures to reach his daughter, my patient admitted that the wall was "very thick" for him to penetrate.

This story presents a clear example of alienation. My patient's mother may not have intended to alienate her daughter from her father. But, after having her child's trust as the primary parent, she had systematically cast aspersions at the father, instilling doubt and fear about him and supporting the daughter's distance without cause.

Similarly, in cases where I have served as a guardian ad litem (court evaluator), I have seen parents influence their children. These matters can be quite complex to sort through. At the same time, more often than not, I find that the views children have regarding their parents are often based on behaviors the children have actually experienced. Yet I have also observed that the claim of alienation is often used as a defense by parents who fail to recognize the legitimate anger their children feel toward them for concrete reasons that the parent cannot really hear.

Yet allegations of alienation or brainwashing are used frequently and, sometimes unfairly, are successfully argued in court. In other cases, as mentioned previously, if the parent who is genuinely protecting his or her child may appeal to the judge by using the argument of alienation or brainwashing, their efforts can backfire and the court can return the child to the alienated parent, perceiving the claim as a ploy. Parents serve both themselves and their child (in addition to their former spouses) by monitoring behaviors that may instill negative attributions of the other parent. Such behaviors may initially create resistance toward the other parent but often, ultimately, create the feeling for the child that he or she was duped by the parent whom the child trusted. By enabling your children to have private exchanges and supporting them to develop the relationship that *they* seek with both parents, you will not be guilty of muddying their relationship with your former spouse and will be able to more confidently support your child's preferences.

For trained evaluators and judges, parental actions become clearer when the case is investigated carefully. The way children and parents report details of seemingly inappropriate incidents is very telling. The "enthusiasm" of a parent to exaggerate information about the other parent or to discuss his or her ex-spouse's antisocial character or personality disorder can be curtailed by careful attention during the interview process of the parents and children in individual and group meetings. Exploration and attentiveness to basic questions usually lead to considerable findings. Questions like the following are crucial:

- How does the parent respond—in words, facial expressions, and body language—to the accusations?
- How does each side relate and interact in joint sessions?
- While parental alienation syndrome is a questionable theory, is it a variable of credible concern for significantly influencing the children?
- Is there substantiated evidence for claims of alienation and brainwashing, or the opposite—evidence explaining the children's resistance toward a parent?

The court formally adjudicates on real evidence—not simply hearsay—to confirm that a child is being forcibly alienated or brainwashed. For example, a parent may advocate for a judgment on the other parent and insist that the children experience the other parent in the same manner, rather than permitting the children to form their own opinions.

It is often evident how such actions distort boundaries and the role of authority in the home. As previously mentioned, attacking one parent can also be construed as an attack against the child—as the child sees both parents as extensions of himself or herself. For those in the position to make decisions regarding the child's welfare, calling out inappropriate behavior of one parent is not only fair but also essential to their role.

SEVERE CIRCUMSTANCES DURING DIVORCE

Many children have suffered as the objects of emotional, sexual, and physical abuse by a parent (often the father), while the other parent did nothing. In the Divorce Study, 52 percent of children reported difficulty managing their parents' divorces due to verbal and physical abuse. In matters of abuse, everyone is at risk. This is partially why it is always appropriate to maintain boundaries that respect the dignity of each member of a home. One of the advantages of a two-parent household is that each parent can provide a check on the management of boundaries, discipline, and actions in the interest of the children. In that case, if there are violations of these boundaries, the other parent sounds the alarm. Not to act—inaction—is action.

In cases of physical, sexual, and emotional abuse, this can be more complicated to assess, since children may feel too intimidated to reveal their experiences. You would need the expert training and assessment skills of a specialist to help your child. Yet, as we've discussed, while the parent claiming alienation or brainwashing may be the perpetrator, both the well-intentioned parent and child can become the victims. And again, the court can place the child in the hands of the abuser.

These reports of parents from the Divorce Study detail unwinnable situations for children of divorce who are caught in the crossfire and are uncertain about whom or what to believe and trust.

> My husband and his attorney derailed this case. It was a clear-cut case of abuse and neglect; and they turned it into "my mental problems." [The] children have been suffering ever since because he brainwashes them. They are confused and do not know who to trust or believe anymore. They feel they have been let down by everyone.
> —Parent (married seven and a half years)

> This has been an extreme divorce and the system here has turned their backs on this situation. . . . My children have suffered as a

result. Even judges have turned their backs to the issue and have said flat-out that they won't deal with any of "that"—meaning all the evidence I laid out as abuse. I worry every minute of every day about how this is affecting them. . . . I still haven't told my youngest son bad things about his father, even though he has alienated the others from me. I explain to him why I am telling him things and only tell him what he needs to know. . . . I don't want him to be manipulated and brainwashed like the others were and are. I don't know if I have done the right thing as no one knows this situation. I hope I have been doing the right thing.

—Parent (married one year)

My ex got custody due to his being financially stable, and not anything that I did wrong. He would never allow me to work or to go to school. He was extremely controlling and abusive. Now he is emotionally and mentally abusive to my daughter. My daughter's therapist has documented this, worked with her for over a year and a half, and now wants to have my daughter removed from my ex-husband's custody so that she can begin supervised visitation. . . . My daughter is acting out more and more. I am extremely worried about her and her future. She has been lied to and pulled constantly by her father; and he does everything he can to keep me from having anything to do with her.

—Parent (married one year)

When you are being misrepresented and maligned in court, it may be difficult to stay focused on your goals and to not get defensive or overwhelmed—particularly if there are additional incentives for attorneys, like financial gain. Children often become allies for their parents in light of the spouse's vacancy and because of their intimate role concerning these issues. Parents feel a need to talk to someone, and who knows the issues more than the children? On rare occasions, the children's stories make them party to the process—as in the case of abuse. Engaging children in the court process places them squarely in the middle.

It is in the best interest of the children that parents who are emotionally or physically abusive are separated from their children, as the harm from abuse is so much greater than that of the divorce alone. In such abusive situations, it is appropriate for children to be cautiously included in court proceedings. Requiring children to interact with and endure abusive parents often causes permanent damage. Consider the following reports from the Divorce Study:

> They no longer live in a world of hate and anger in my home or see me get hit or belittled; but I had to put orders of protection on him and he still violated them. Through all of this, I could never get the court to see him for what he was and still had to send them there for visits, which were harmful and kept them in limbo. I called the Department of Family Services at least three times to try to get them away; but they just always told me it was poor judgment and not abuse. They were wrong.
>
> —*Parent (married fourteen years)*

> Their father continued to hurt me through our kids, by playing legal games and visitation games. His sister went along with him by trying to tell our son that I do not love him and never wanted him, which is totally untrue. . . . My son suffers in silence because he has been subjected to coercive brainwashing and he has endured a lot of lies and is not sure what is true and what is not anymore. . . . My daughter has not learned some of the social skills she should have; and her dad has told her since she was young "there is something wrong with you, it's genetic, from your mother." My daughter went from not believing it (thinking he says that when he's angry) to now believing it.
>
> —*Parent (married one year)*

Knowing that whatever I said would be used against the other parent in court has left me never wanting to make a decision or speak up. I would just go along with whatever the parent I was talking to wanted.

—*Twenty-five-year-old (age two at the time of divorce)*

In time, as children grow into adults, they may seek out more information so they are better able to understand what occurred to cause their parents' divorce. This information should be shared as needed for their well-being, understanding, and growth, but not for the therapeutic benefit of the parents.

PARENTAL RECOMMENDATIONS

Here are seven ways you can revitalize your children's ability to trust during and after divorce:

1. *Commit to your children through your actions, not just your words.* Among the most basic and vital things violated by divorce is commitment. Divorce breaks the central tenet of a marital vow. As if mimicking Hollywood weddings that cost millions of dollars but are all show and no substance, we have come to expect that these models of modern life tell you that you can toss marriage away. The commitment of marriage sometimes lasts just months, weeks, or even days. The media focuses too much attention on empty celebrity marriages that end seemingly right after they've begun, providing children with a perception of marriage as disposable. This, along with children's firsthand experience of divorce, affects their perception of marriage and trust. In turn, this renders children at risk for intergenerationally transmitted divorce. **Parents must**

rebuild their children's trust by coming through in every way possible, not only through words—as children have learned that words are often meaningless—but also by actions and behaviors.

2. *Practice healthy communication.* Your children have probably seen full-length demonstrations of poor communication preceding, during, and following your divorce, both through marital disagreements and finalizing the legality of the divorce. But consider asking yourself:

   - When interacting with my ex-spouse, other adults, and my children, do I communicate effectively by exhibiting good listening skills and sound reasoning?
   - How do my kids feel when I communicate with them?
   - Do I intimidate my children? How do they characterize me?
   - Are my emotional responses overreactive and overwhelming for my children?
   - Do my children feel comfortable opening up to me?
   - Do I respond to my children's needs by paying attention to what they convey through their words and actions?

   You may find that the best way to initiate communication—if good rapport is not in place—is to enter into your child's world of concern and interests in order to create genuine exchanges, all while being mindful of how to respond appropriately. Are you in touch with your children's worlds, hopes, dreams, and desires?

3. *When they are ready, help your children process their hurt and pain.* In therapy, children of divorce have often shared with me that many nights they cried themselves to sleep because no one was there for them. Conversely, some children did not cry, but cut themselves because it was the only way for them to feel. As the Divorce Study confirmed, children have been pained by divorce. Always be cognizant of your children's needs and ask yourself, *Am I there for my children?* **You must be able to connect emotionally to your children. Allow them to share**

feelings, acknowledge their concerns, address your own feelings, and always affirm and express care. Reinforce the belief that your children can depend on you.

4. *Build connections through fun and positive energy.* Divorce is not fun or enjoyable. However, this does not change the fact that kids want to be kids. Though it may get an initial rise from them, showering your children with gifts, toys, and trips is not the way to create fun and positive energy and relationships. Parents must initiate positive energy, which invites a shared experience. This is an opportunity for bonding and creating a connection with your children, discussed further in chapter 9. **You want to replace the loss that children feel during divorce and create a home filled with inspiration through spontaneous joy and happiness.**

5. *Be both physically and emotionally present.* If a parent exits a child's life—much as Megan described in her poem, "When the Sidewalk Ends"—a bottomless pit often overshadows a child's existence. Children in the Divorce Study often expressed that it would have been easier to manage the death of their parent than endure the divorce. The unknown arrangements and potential of losing loved ones are often a child's greatest fear. **Work to counter that feeling of abandonment by knowing that your children feel your presence. Be there whenever possible.** Parents who lose custody may say this is easier said than done. I cannot imagine a more agonizing situation than finding that your child has built an impenetrable wall to keep you out.

6. *Help your children manage their fears.* How can children not feel anxious and cautious after enduring their parents' divorce? Children of divorce have been exposed to significant pain and hurt, if not a full-blown trauma. Your children have every reason not to let anyone get too close; they don't want to feel the pain they observed in a so-called loving relationship. They are constantly waiting for the other shoe to drop. **To**

prevent anxiety and overcautiousness, work to foster peace and harmony through interactions where you exhibit understanding and create calm.

7. *Love your children unconditionally.* Most children cannot imagine not loving their parents unconditionally forever. But beware; hate can play out in divorce if children perceive not only their parents' lack of love for each other but also their lack of love for the children. They may lose their trust in love altogether. Following divorce, **words will not suffice to repair the damage.** Instead, demonstrating care and love may help combat the negativity your children experience. **You can find time to explain how your understanding of commitment, trust, and unconditional love failed in your marriage, but, more important, you need to act in ways that redeem your relationship with your children.**

For kids to trust their parents during and after a divorce, adults must walk the walk and be honest with their children, who are quite skillful at picking up deceitful and contradictory behavior. When parents fail to meet their children's needs during divorce—as presented with Megan's story—they may have to work much harder to win back confidence that was lost; lost trust from a parent constitutes a deep injury. Sadly, if trust is not reestablished, children can develop trust issues that disable their parental relationships and affect intimate relationships for the rest of their lives. Parents can counteract those feelings by being honest and compassionate, sharing facts that serve the interest of the children but do not cross the line of overexposing them.

In chapter 7, we will walk through your children's development stage-by-stage so that you can provide age-appropriate responses to their needs.

Chapter 7

REDEFINE PARENTING

Yes, I wanted an opportunity to show them I am still the same dad who took them fishing, played games, went on vacations, had home barbeques, went to church with them, cheered them on at sporting events, tucked them in bed at night, got them up in the mornings, cooked them breakfast, took them to school, worked on school projects and homework, and was there for school activities.

—PARENT (MARRIED TWO YEARS)

Parental Oversight 7

Parents may be tempted to look for quick, one-size-fits-all solutions for helping their kids through the chaos, but strategies tailored to the children's unique situations will ultimately prove far more effective. Each child who experiences divorce will react in a different way, based on his or her age, developmental stage, personality, and specific family circumstances.

> I think the fact that my dad left us and that we did not have a constant father figure in our lives is the reason why I sought love from various men later on. I feel that divorce affects children in some way, shape, or form. But if the parents love you and really make it known that you are number one and safe and loved by them, then

you can be successful in a marriage so that your own kids can have
two parents.

—Thirty-eight-year-old (age two at the time of divorce)

I get easily upset and don't like crying in front of people. So I didn't
say anything to my parents. I just went to my room and became
distant from everyone.

—Sixteen-year-old (age seven at the time of divorce)

Parents: You don't know who your children are. They smile and act
happy a lot; but they may be sad and just want someone to talk to.
We teens fake smiles a lot.

—Fourteen-year-old (age thirteen at the time of divorce)

When Joan came to me, she didn't need me to tell her that she had
become a poor role model for her kids following her divorce. She already
knew it. Her children were aware of her romantic engagement with one
of her extramarital liaisons. Joan sought my counseling because she
feared that her custody rights were in danger. She admitted to having
affairs, engaging in substance abuse, and "acting adolescent." Joan was
self-aware, but her inability to control her impulses had become a serious
problem for her.

This bright and successful businesswoman with an Ivy League education had a five-year-old daughter and a four-year-old son. She admitted
to abusing drugs and engaging in sexual escapades while the children
were in her care, though her husband had not caught on to Joan's double
life. She confessed that she was narcissistic and immature and felt incapable of changing her behavior.

Joan had grown up in a wealthy family with a psychotic mother and
an absent father. She lacked healthy role models, and now her acting-out
behaviors were being passed on to her own children. The circumstances
of every family touched by divorce are unique. Joan had two young

children, a troubled history with her own parents, and issues with drugs and sex. Healing the brokenness in her family would require a completely different set of strategies than I would suggest for a father of teenagers or for older parents with adult children.

I worked with Joan to help her understand the impact of her broken family of origin and to implement responsible parenting techniques through healthy actions that met her children's specific developmental and emotional needs. Regretfully, I cannot offer the same personalized advice to each of my readers. I can, however, offer insight as to what challenges a typical child at a given age may encounter when faced with parents who are no longer together.

THE SPECIFIC NEEDS OF YOUR CHILDREN FROM INFANCY TO LATE ADOLESCENCE

As discussed previously, parents going through a divorce frequently forget to differentiate between their own needs and those of their children. Developmental psychologists explain that a child's life unfolds as he or she meets a series of challenges through each stage of growth. The challenges rely on the child's readiness to confront them, based on his or her successful navigation of each stage.

For example, child psychologist Erik Erikson explained that infants experience their world as trusting or untrusting ("trust versus mistrust") based on the quality and consistency of their parental care. Regardless of how infants resolve this first-stage challenge (whether or not they feel that they can trust their parents or their world), they move to the next challenge. As toddlers, they proceed to confront the next challenge of "autonomy versus shame." During this stage, they address their independence and autonomy.[1] When children are encouraged and supported, they develop confidence and security; if overcontrolled and criticized, they feel insecure and inadequate, and they lack self-esteem. Erikson defined six more stages or "psychosocial crises" that we confront throughout the life cycle that render our sense of efficacy. Because divorce disrupts the flow of nurturing support that facilitates this process—especially prior to adulthood—children can find it difficult to master effectively their developmental challenges.[2] Divorce interrupts children in distinct ways at each point of their early developmental challenges, which affects their adult growth and development.

Most parents recognize that their children have different needs depending on their ages, and they intuitively address those needs. It is also important to consider the temperament and personal needs of your child as *you* respond to their emotional concerns.[3] Let's consider the specific needs children have, based on their development stages and the challenge divorce presents to the tasks they must accomplish.

1. Infancy

Though your infant cannot understand what is transpiring, babies feel the tension that often accompanies divorce. This *sensory-motor stage* allows them to understand their world through their senses, to communicate their emotional needs physically. If tension affects infants, they are prone to becoming irritable and clingy, expressing emotional outbursts, and possibly even regressing or showing signs of developmental delay. Psychologists recognize that the bonds of trust that develop during infancy occur because of the quality of physical and emotional care provided to the children. When this stage occurs at a time when trust is in jeopardy because of a failing relationship, you must maintain *balanced* engagements (neither overindulging nor undercompensating) for your child and create loving bonds through consistent acts of care. For example, bond during feeding rituals, through interactive communication that occurs during play, and while engaging your baby with positive verbal expressions of love and affection.

To best address the impact of divorce, maintain a consistent routine. This helps to reassure an infant of your presence. This is especially true regarding sleeping, eating, and other structured events like naps. Avoid anxious and highly emotional reactions with your child—whether these are related to the child, the divorce, or other stressors. Setting aside time for holding, comforting, and playing with your child may provide balance for you and your infant. It is critical to be alert and available when your infant seeks attention. In addition, recognize clinginess and try to identify the source of your child's cries so that you can respond effectively.

> [The divorce] made me very insecure about myself. I have very low self-esteem; and I never extend myself in relationships with the opposite sex because I am afraid to make the same mistakes my parents made. I don't want to bring children into a world that is not good.
>
> —*Thirty-seven-year-old (an infant at the time of divorce)*

2. Eighteen Months to Three Years Old

Toddlers seek out their parents to bond with them. Because toddlers are developmentally self-focused, they may perceive that they caused the disruption in their parents' lives—even though the concept of divorce is too complicated for them to understand. Crying and other manipulative behaviors may evolve. Your child's distress may be expressed through attention seeking, crying, thumb sucking, and neglect of toilet training. Actual fear of abandonment can be expressed through difficulty sleeping or fear of sleeping alone.

To respond to the impact of divorce, parents may create schedules in which their children can spend quality time with both parents. Extra time can ease the fears your child experiences. Engaging in activities, such as games or reading, is encouraged. It's essential to make time to discuss in simple terms the plan for your divorce in order to include them and respond to their reactions appropriately. Often, children display their fears when going to bed and while asleep (through their dreams and nightmares). In response to arguments and distress that they may be exposed to, they require your reassurance and support so they can be assured that they are not in danger and can count on your love.

Even before my divorce, I had a general policy for managing fears at night, fears that understandably reemerged for my children when their anxiety intruded on their sleep during my divorce. My children knew that they were welcome in my bedroom from a very young age; they were allowed to bring in their comforters and pillows and get comfortable on the floor, as they felt the need. Though they hadn't done this for some time, they camped out in this way more frequently during the period around the divorce. They could decide when they did not want to be alone, and I retained an open-door policy so they knew they did not have to sleep alone—to know that they were not physically alone when they felt uncomfortable or uneasy. Often we would discuss their decision, and, eventually, they returned to their own rooms in their own time. The message here is be responsive and available to address your children's fears and meet their needs.

The protests of children can be daunting. Little children often protest out of an effort to assert themselves, to express discomfort, or for no apparent reason at all. Your ability to respond constructively and positively is critical in conveying security during this transition. Becoming hostile or overreacting to the child's distressful behavior will make a difficult situation more disturbing for you and emotionally painful for them. Your resolve and kindness will ultimately win in most interactions with your children. Keep in mind, however, that there may be many variables in the mix of their rejection and lack of willingness to conform, such as their discomfort with changes to their rituals resulting from the divorce. Do your best. You must permit yourself to rest with security and not let your children's reactions govern or direct your studied judgment.

> [My parents] had no clue back then about how the impact of their actions affected their children—even as toddlers. I can remember as a little child crawling in a fetal position and in my mind making myself shrink to make the yelling and screaming go away.
>
> —*Fifty-one-year-old ("too young" to remember the time of divorce)*

3. Three to Six Years Old

Preschool-aged children will understand more about the loss of divorce and will most likely not want their parents to divorce. Given the number of reminders children need at this age, they may feel that they caused the problems leading to the divorce. They may interpret that they caused the "game" to end by failing to do something. They are more self-aware, which leaves them prone to nightmares and feelings of guilt and distress.

While these children are beginning to define their choices, they tend to be indecisive. When talking with their mothers, they may say, "I want to be with Mommy," and when talking with their fathers, they may say, "I want to live with Daddy." Several of my patients who have toddlers who are no longer living with the other parent describe how, after the dust settles from the day's activities, their children become fussy and cranky, throw tantrums, and struggle to sleep in response to the absence of the other parent. They simply don't want their parents to divorce! At this age, children have feelings but do not necessarily understand them.

In response to the divorce, your preschooler will have thoughts, feelings, and many questions. Be sure you've told them you are available to talk. This doesn't mean saying, "I'm available," but it *does* mean recognizing that if you're not actively spending time with and talking with your preschooler, you probably are not really available. By establishing respectful interactions with your ex-spouse, you will communicate that your child is not losing either of his or her parents, but is making adjustments because of your divorce. Phone calls and check-ins can be helpful, but they are sometimes stressful, since these communications can cause anxiety for parents who are going through a contentious divorce. Nonetheless, when parents call or check in with their children, they should respect their kids' privacy and confidentiality. Children want to feel at ease and encouraged to share what is going on in their lives or express their personal sentiments with the parent calling. Recognizing that this is not always possible—as divorces are not easily managed—you will want to work with the other parent to establish a routine of visitation or engagement that makes the transition as seamless as possible.

To this day, I've never been a person who can show emotion easily; and I think a lot of that stems from harboring feelings as a young- ster and not wanting to show either parent that I was hurt out of fear of hurting them. It's amazing how things very early in your life can follow you.

—*Twenty-nine-year-old (age five at the time of divorce)*

4. Six to Eleven Years Old

Identification with the parent of the same sex as the child is espe- cially significant during pre-adolescence, particularly for children who have had a positive experience of family life. Their fear of abandon- ment and loss will be much more acute as they understand more about the consequences or changes that will affect them as a result of their parents' divorce. Sometimes children have such a difficult time accept- ing the divorce that they will create stories about their parents getting back together—and they certainly may wish for this. As the thoughts and feelings of children at this age become more complex, the neces- sary adjustment they must make is more complicated. If their needs are unmet, they are prone to act out.

For boys, acting out usually manifests itself through angry behav- iors, while girls tend to internalize or withdraw. For example, boys may pick fights or become more physically aggressive and reactive; girls tend to suppress their feelings and internalize their anger, not showing their pain or being detectably irritable. Depression and anxiety are also observed in both pre-adolescent boys and girls, stemming from signifi- cant feelings of sadness, fear, and hurt. If these behaviors occur, your child deserves your attention and professional support.[4]

I have experienced bouts of depression and have struggled with an anxiety disorder that I try to keep in check, without being on medication. I was on antidepressants, antianxiety meds, and sleeping meds throughout my twenties.

—*Thirty-eight-year-old (age eight at the time of divorce)*

You can counter the blow to your child's self-esteem by developing a more personal relationship with them. Make time for day trips, and do not only attend their games but also spend special, quality time with each of your children, individually, pursuing their interests with them. In this way, you demonstrate your genuine support and availability. This encourages your children to feel safe, to open up, and to express their thoughts and feelings. Listening carefully is important, and responding to their questions and concerns—to the best of your ability—is essential. Working to keep your children on track and in a routine will instill secure feelings. Your support in this way will be deeply appreciated. Your child recognizes that this is a very hard time for you as well. **Giving your children the courage to stay focused on their interests and possibilities will convey that you are okay and that their lives do not have to be put on hold.**

5. Early Adolescence: Eleven to Fourteen Years Old

Children form their own opinions during early adolescence. Depending on the connections they have established at home, they may be aligned with confidantes or act totally remote. The work of your earlier parenting years begins to bear fruit during adolescence. Many of my neighbors and the parents of my children's friends take it as an indisputable fact that parents cannot relate to their teenage children. I do not recall this experience. If you provide reasonable counsel, your children will relate to you. Of course, all adolescents face unique challenges that require some space for exploration, including learning from trial and error and making developmental adjustments. Adolescence is a tumultuous time for young people confronting challenges laden with changes in their biological, intellectual, moral, emotional, sexual, social, and spiritual development. So there may be a period or two when it's difficult to reach them. Resist imposing your *official authority* by only enforcing rules, and you will inspire *authentic authority* through your sensitivity, understanding guidance, and caring support. With these interventions you will strengthen their confidence and your relationship with them.

At this stage, children are more prone to getting into serious trouble, whether through self-harm, substance abuse, or problems with psychological adjustment. Be sure not to sell yourself or your children short. Provide clear guidance, and also preserve and develop a respectful relationship with your adolescents so they can recognize you as a proven and valued counsel rather than merely an enforcer of dated rules.

> I did not speak about [the divorce to my parents] because they wouldn't let me. They told me that it didn't affect me because I was young and would get over it.
>
> —*Fifteen-year-old (age fifteen at the time of divorce)*

To counteract the negative implications of divorce, respond as patiently as possible to your adolescent. Children need to take time to process what divorce entails and how it affects them.

Divorce raises even more challenges for parents when their children do not believe that they can understand their needs or make time for them. This often widens the gap between parents and children and leads children to turn to other, potentially undesirable sources of attention and support. If you maintain your role as trusted counsel, they will recognize that you understand their questions and can help them sort out solutions. This will be useful to your children not only during the divorce but also during other times in their lives as they respond to social situations and pressures, including sexuality, drugs, and community interactions.

Enter your children's world by asking pertinent questions and discussing real issues. You can use your own discretion when discussing your divorce, but keep in mind that this is not an opportunity to share your war stories but instead an opening to assist your children grappling with their developmental challenges.

6. Later Adolescence: Fifteen to Eighteen Years Old

In later adolescence, children begin to envision their adult identities and build foundations for their transition into adulthood—from driving a car to pursuing a career. Keep in mind that they are not yet adults and still require adult support and contact. While your presence is not the central factor in your teen's world, your home should continue to function as his or her home. Your children may not want to have you as their Saturday night date, but they should still value their time with you. If you have created a genuine relationship with your children where they can discuss their views, desires, and interests, your investment in their lives will be invaluable.

To respond to the impact of divorce, engage with your children during their adolescence so they know you are really available, want to understand, and genuinely care. Permissive parenting, as described in chapter 3, is a common trap for parents going through divorce. These parents may leave their children unsupervised, confirming their teens' sense of abandonment and unimportance—which levies a strong blow to their self-esteem. Without guidance, it is difficult for children to move forward with their personal and professional lives.

> I don't think I was the cause of the divorce; but my older sister does feel responsible to this day. My parents never told her she was the cause; but they were very hard on her. They fought a lot about parenting, and she seemed to get the brunt of it. She ran away (across the country) for six months when she was fifteen years old.
>
> *—Forty-four-year-old (age twelve at the time of divorce)*

There are many styles of parenting, as we previously considered in chapter 3; however, effective parenting requires aligning your temperament and your child's needs. Parents need to provide homes where children receive guidance, direction, and love; most important, the atmosphere needs to be one that is inviting, comfortable, and child friendly. What children receive in their homes needs to be treated as precious and invaluable. By maintaining structure in the home and checking in with your kids to determine whether their needs are met, you ensure that their home life is meaningful and that family ties stay strong. Children of divorce, who have witnessed disruption and had their sense of family and home violated, are especially in need of this type of connection in their lives.

Just as you have special needs during divorce, your children do as well. The positive side of this is that if those needs are identified, an effective response and resolution is possible on your part. Seek resources from others who are in a position to guide you with these matters. A school counselor, teacher, coach, clergyman, therapist, and others are trained to give you readings on your children's performance and the quality of their social engagement. Be alert to emotional cues from your children. It is understandable that they have negative feelings about the divorce. But you can discern the impact the divorce is having on them by observing how they manage their emotions, feelings, and actions. You must keep the doors open for addressing their needs and providing support. There are few greater joys in life than parents watching their children take flight. Take ownership of your parenting to enable your children to be fully alive and to soar!

7. Your Children as Adults

You have read that several respondents to the Divorce Study had strong negative feelings about their parents' divorce for many years (even decades) after the breakup of their families. Regardless of his or her age, you are always a parent to your child. Grown adults may be better able to intellectually understand the reasons for your divorce, but they may have multiple levels of thoughts and feelings that lead them to perceive strengths and weaknesses in both parents, as well as feelings of deep personal loss and sadness. Permit your adult children to have their own minds, and recognize that you may view things differently and they may remain conflicted about your decision to divorce. Accepting their differences in opinion demonstrates your respect for your adult children's points of view and provides the opportunity for positive growth in your relationship.

My parents hurt me deeply by not showing me love or affection, or giving me advice or encouragement. It had nothing to do with the divorce. It was just that way. I did not become aware of my feelings about my childhood until I was an adult, although I vividly remember hating my mother at age twelve and counting down the days until I turned eighteen.

—*Fifty-two-year-old (age twelve at the time of divorce)*

BOB AND KAREN'S STORY

Bob and Karen agreed that they wanted an amicable divorce, minimizing conflict and disruption in the lives of their children. Before they told their six-year-old, Brenda, and eight-year-old, Cory, about the breakup, they worked out their divorce plans, including their property and custody agreements, all in great detail. Both were already involved with other partners, whom they would eventually marry.

After their careful preparation, Bob and Karen sat down with their young son and daughter and calmly explained that they still cared for each other and loved their children but thought it was best to divorce each other, as they had grown apart in their relationship.

The two children were baffled by the expressions of mutual affection; even kids as young as Cory and Brenda knew that divorce was "a bad thing." When Brenda and Cory stared at them in confusion, their parents assured them that everything would be all right, and that they would soon have new stepsiblings and new homes where they would be happy and peaceful.

I met Cory when he was a sophomore in college. Strikingly, it was because of his parents' "amicable" divorce that he felt he suffered from social anxiety and insecurity. He said that his family's changes left him unable to form relationships. When I asked him how his parents' divorce created his anxiety, he broke down in tears, crying uncontrollably, and said, "No one ever asked me what I felt."

Once he composed himself, Cory explained that his parents' effort to create the "perfect" divorce had not included an effort to help him deal with his feelings about the breakup of his family. "They never asked what I thought about what was happening."

Cory's parents had acted conscientiously to give him what *they* thought he needed. However, they made the mistake of never asking *him* what he needed.

As a psychologist, I am experienced in recognizing distress signals from my patients. As a father, I was alert to the emotions and behaviors of my own children during my divorce and sought to help discover constructive paths.

My son, Anthony, was eleven years old and had always been quick to smile, joke around, and laugh. Upon learning of our divorce, Anthony's demeanor shifted dramatically. His generative and fluid humor faded, and his mood darkened. His playfulness and joy changed to withdrawal and sadness. I was alarmed at how rapidly my son descended into the depths of grief.

These are usual reactions to the turmoil children feel. Children—as well as their parents—often go through the same stages of grief during a divorce as those that follow a death in the family. The classic stages of working through death—denial, anger, bargaining, depression, and acceptance—are common experiences during a divorce. The sequence can change, and in Anthony's case, he reached depression quickly after recognizing that his efforts and hopes for saving my relationship with his mother would not be successful. Anger soon followed, and he eventually came to acceptance.

It is a poor assumption to believe your children can act as you prefer—for example, expecting them to feel happy and that everything is all right. Nor does it help to say things like, "I want the old Anthony back." You have to allow them to process their feelings and experiences through their own unique expressions of grief. This does not mean that you should remain morose or indulge in their negative feelings. As the

Divorce Study revealed, 74 percent of parents felt regret about the negative impact their divorce had on their children.

This is not to suggest that you should passively accept your children's pain. You have the ability to prevent these statistical realities by respecting and listening to your children's feelings. Then they'll know they have a confidant who is present and available to better their lives.

Children are entitled to their feelings and should not be led to pretend, inauthentic emotional responses. Ease your children's distress and encourage them at every possible opportunity to hold on to normalcy in the regular activities that they enjoy.

Playing hockey was one of my son's favorite pastimes. At first, it took more effort to get him to practices and games during the initial turmoil of the divorce, but it was worth it. Getting myself to each of those games allowed me to cheer him on and see him reclaim his force. I made this a priority because playing hockey gave my son some assurance that his whole world was not falling apart. It helped him retain his footing in the world of "normal" and to experience success and access his joy.

Similarly, my eldest daughter is a competitive figure skater, and she has often described skating as her sanctuary. This description conveyed the reality that regardless of my efforts to minimize my children's exposure to the divorce, sparks were flying, and these were poignantly experienced. On the ice, my daughter was able to find a state of inner peace. My youngest found dance, cheerleading, and academic studies to be valuable and creative outlets for directing her energy and working constructively through her feelings, all while experiencing support.

Parental Recommendations

You may feel that your ability to be a positive example has taken a hit since your relationship ended, and perhaps you struggle to understand why. Many divorcing couples admit that they do not know how to parent or that they neglect their duties or responsibilities during the trauma of divorce.

> My children were five and seven at the time of the divorce. Looking back on it, I had *no idea* what I was doing. I tried to factor in the children, but nothing really prepares someone for seeing their children hurt, confused, and scared, because of choices that we were making to divorce.
>
> —*Parent (married ten years)*

> As much as I felt at the time, with hindsight being what it is, perhaps I (we) could have done more to help them understand. But how could we really?
>
> —*Parent (married thirteen years)*

> The children's father and I were separated four times before we divorced. The first time for over a year. And we still tried to make it work for the children's sake. When the final end came and he got his own place, at first the children wanted to go spend the night with him. When I began to see the toll it took on them and truly understood their loss of security, I did everything I could to lessen the impact. The eye-opener for me was when I heard them talking about mommy's house and daddy's house and realized they no longer felt like they had a home of their own.
>
> —*Parent (married eight years)*

Regardless of what has happened in the past, it's not too late to provide your children with the guidance they need. For best results, keep these principles in mind:

- *Acknowledge that your family's situation is unique and that what works for another family might not work for you.* While all parents are tasked with providing their children with direction, responding to their children's concerns, and effectively listening and communicating, you will need to figure out what that looks like in your family.

Children express themselves uniquely regarding divorce. Because your divorce has a significant impact on your children's lives, you will want to pay attention to the way they cope with the changes and ensure that the guidance you provide them is the kind needed to support your relationship with them. Your children may even work hard to shield you from their genuine feelings. Additionally, younger children may not have the ability to articulate their feelings verbally. That is why paying close attention to them is so crucial.

- *Recognize each child's individual personality, needs, and challenges, and develop a plan that meets each of your children where her or she is.* As the parent, you are in the best position to help your children access their passions, engage their creativity, and find their paths to fulfillment. It is not enough to tell your children what sort of adults you want them to become; you will find it more helpful to show them by modeling behaviors that prove that they have value and that they are loved and worthy of that love.

- *Regularly check in with your kids about their emotional states, even when they become adult children of divorce.* Being conscientious and vigilant about your children's emotional state is one of the most critical parental responsibilities. Listening to your children can be a gut- and heart-wrenching experience. They will say things you don't agree with. They will confront you and even disempower your authority and role. They will question your behavior and your trustworthiness. They may even reenact the behaviors of your spouse with you. They will slap you with the truth of *their* experiences. They may even break down in tears in front of you. It's very easy to miss important warning signs. But only you know your own unique children. You do not want to ignore their feelings or simply assume that you've put their fears to rest. Work hard to practice unconditional love; this love will prevail in the end.

Chapter 8 presents concerns that parents and children of divorce face when they embark on another common stage of relational evolution following divorce: merging family members through new marital relationships and establishing a blended family.

Chapter 8

RETAIN YOUR PARENTHOOD
IN A BLENDED FAMILY

Being in a blended family when I was a child actually helped me to realize what it takes to keep a marriage strong. I'm in a situation now where I'm a stepmom. So my experience has been helpful in realizing what children are going through. I know that they have similar feelings to what I had when I was young.

—Twenty-six-year-old (age five at the time of divorce)

Parental Oversight 8

It is not uncommon for divorced parents to remarry, believing that a new marriage will bring stability and happiness and will help resolve past problems for the entire family, including the children. For many children, however, living with new stepparents and stepsiblings requires a big adjustment, and it can be challenging. Children often feel as though their importance to their parent has been lessened to make way for the new family structure.

> They never asked how we were feeling. They expected us to get over it, move on, and accept what they did next. They expected us

to be resilient and accept their new lifestyles, spouses, and all that comes with a blended family.

—Fifty-five-year-old (age nineteen at the time of divorce)

My mother's financial instability put my sister and me in dangerous situations with inappropriate people (babysitters, roommates, boyfriends). Also, my mother's second husband was abusive. Part of his hold on her was her worry about how she would support us if she did in fact leave him. As far as my relationship with my father, it has never been close. I tend not to trust men in general; and he was the first imprint of that pattern for me. My sister and I suffered enormous abuse at the hands of our stepfather, and my dad never even asked if we were okay. He just wasn't there.

—Forty-four-year-old (age three at the time of divorce)

When my mom remarried, I felt forced to deny the importance of my biological dad in my life.

—Twenty-seven-year-old (age three at the time of divorce)

Once my dad got remarried, everything changed. My brother and I were made to feel like second-class citizens in comparison to our stepsister. The things that mattered to me really didn't matter to them; and they didn't take care of us like they should have.

—Thirty-year-old (age eight at the time of divorce)

Statistics reveal that somewhere between 45 and 50 percent of first marriages end in divorce, 67 to 70 percent of second marriages fail, and third marriages reveal an even grimmer picture of a 73 to 75 percent failure rate.[1]

These facts are not surprising when we consider the care required to maintain quality relationships, and the complexities from more and more variables, factors, and people being introduced into the family. That is, the more marriages one has, the more likely it is that one will accumulate more ex-spouses, stepchildren, and other family members— all of whom become a part of an individual's extended family.

> I was expected to feel nothing but happiness, according to my mother. I would cry when I would see my father because I wanted a life with him. I couldn't let him see me cry because he said it made him feel bad and that was why he didn't come see me more often . . . because I cried.
>
> —*Forty-seven-year-old (age ten at the time of divorce)*

> I had no real example of a father. I lived with my grandparents with my mom, and grandpa was great in helping to raise me; but it was never a father-daughter relationship. My father was the worst example of a father. So, I was always getting hurt by him.
>
> —*Twenty-eight-year-old (age two at the time of divorce)*

> I'm thankful that I have my stepmom and my mom; but it would have been nice to have a better relationship with my mom. Now, growing up with my dad, I see I'm nothing like her—all my morals and values pretty much are all the same as my dad's.
>
> —*Eighteen-year-old (age five at the time of divorce)*

By their very nature, blended families face multiple challenges, including

- parenting styles
- finances
- daily rituals, as well as religious and spiritual traditions (like holidays)
- role expectations
- boundaries

If we consider the familial challenges and sibling rivalries of an intact family, how much more complex might these be within a blended family? In this chapter, we will identify some of the major adjustments confronted when parents and children become part of a new family unit.

Let's return to the story of Maya, introduced in chapter 1, who described her struggle to understand her parents' divorce and to express her feelings. The rest of Maya's story follows, highlighting the challenges of blended families—from her changing relationship with her mother and the discord she experienced with her stepfather to the profound influence of her stepmother on her life.

Maya's Story (Part 2)

I was only a toddler when my mother remarried. My mom and stepfather had frequent date nights; and my stepfather ruled the household with an iron fist. Despite him being in our lives as far back as I can remember, it took some time for my brother and me to adjust to our stepfather's presence. For example, he frequently insisted that our bedrooms be "spotless." If there were a toy or piece of clothing where it shouldn't have been, he would ransack our bedrooms and demand we clean things up until they were "right." My stepfather required that we follow his rules, or we would be spanked with a "walnut paddle"—his designated instrument for enforcing discipline. Spankings and disagreements were frequent, especially as my brother and I grew older and struggled to maintain a relationship with our biological father.

I often complained to my mother. She was willing to discuss my concerns about my stepfather, but, more often than not, she would side with him. On one occasion, I asked her, "Which relationship was your highest priority, your children or your marriage?" She promptly answered, her marriage. I was flabbergasted and, more significantly, deeply hurt by her response.

The day my half brother was born marked a complete household shift. At this point, my authoritative stepfather discovered a side of tenderness and nurturance. The spankings and demands dwindled as his love for my half brother grew. My mother maintained her diplomatic parenting approach and didn't seem nearly as affected by my half brother's birth as my stepfather, who was enamored by his every breath. What's striking is that my stepfather's first priority was his family, while my mother's priority was her marriage.

In time, my stepfather and I were able to develop a relationship based on trust and kindness, rather than fear and control. It wasn't until my early twenties that I understood why my mother valued her marriage above all else: it was to uphold the value she had in relationships and to meet her needs, in order to ultimately provide for her family. These familial resolutions validated my place within my family and the worth I so longed for.

—*Twenty-five-year-old (age six months at the time of divorce)*

Maya shared with me that her parents held joint custody. Soon after her parents' divorce, her father met a lovely woman and created a home with her. His strong desire to make his new relationship work led Maya's father to financially overextend himself and purchase a large home with a mortgage that required working long hours. He became increasingly stressed. Maya and her brother rarely saw their father, who fell into a depression. Those stresses and her father's depression ultimately led to her father's divorce from his second wife. Yet Maya established and retained a deep relationship with her stepmother, whom Maya viewed as genuinely caring and who guided her stepdaughter lovingly. Maya described her stepmother as "highly trustworthy, kind, and gentle, fostering her passions and creativity—a real caretaker."

Another nurturing resource for Maya in her early development was the close relationships she established with both sets of grandparents. Though Maya was not able to establish deep connections with her father or stepfather, or a strong bond with her mother, she was able to enjoy nurturing and supportive relationships with her grandparents. These relationships enabled her to develop confidence in herself and experience positive male figures in her life.

Her older brother, however, was not as fortunate. He, too, was unable to bond with both his father and his stepfather. Maya recognized that her brother went outside the family to seek meaningful connections, and he fell in with a bad crowd.

The first seven years of Maya's life with her stepfather—before her half brother was born—were difficult, and the stress at home distanced Maya from her mother. Her father's third wife was very involved in her faith. When Maya's dad adopted this new faith, all of his previous interests, including Maya and her brother, became secondary.

Maya continued to retain close contact with her first stepmom, but would soon find herself in yet another family system as her father remarried—this time to a woman with three teenaged children of her own. As her father sought to adjust to his new relationship by sharing in his third wife's pious faith and attending to her children, both Maya and her brother grew even more distant from him.

Maya described a story of different priorities and goals from various family members. Her mother's goal was to secure a family because she had not felt this was possible in her first marriage. For Maya's stepfather, the goal was to create a new family. However, he wanted to shape the family according to his own vision. He was not interested in the uniqueness of his stepchildren. For Maya—as with most children—her goal was to be nurtured and supported so that she could grow into a vital, confident woman.

Maya's story reveals several common complications and challenges that arise as blended families evolve following divorce. First and foremost, the original family structure collapsed. In Maya's case, her stepfather appeared to be an unchallenged interloper, intruding on the children's

Figure 3. Most Influential Characters in Maya's Story

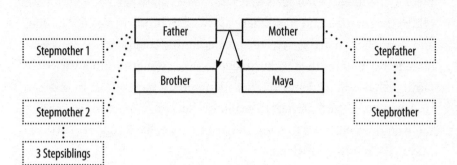

space as their mother passively endured his intrusion in order to meet her larger goal of establishing a family for herself. Stepparents are often put in awkward positions. They enter the inner family circle but remain, by definition, one "step" away from the central role. A good general principle is that stepparents provide support to members of the family but do not take control or dominate, as Maya's stepfather did. They need to defer to the wishes of the biological parent—as they are not blood relatives to the children—unless situations become extreme. Intrusions from stepparents understandably provoke emotional reactions from children.

When discussing the tension in her family, Maya explained that she and her brother enjoyed a cohesive bond with her mother and stepfather's family once their mom and stepfather had a child. Maya's story details the ways in which her life became increasingly complex. The complications occurred as a result of the difficulty that she and her brother faced when trying to access nurturing and support during their development. This required them to expend significant energy on multiple levels, including emotionally and financially, because there were no other resources especially available for and directed at them.

Children must develop bonds with family members who will support them. Maya's capability, character, and path led her to negotiate relationships with each of her various family members, most successfully creating bonds with her grandparents and her stepmother from her

father's second marriage. These bonds were crucial to Maya's development. Other bonds evolved as Maya learned to share parts of herself with
others (her mother and stepfather). Maya's half brother from her mother
and stepfather's marriage created greater family cohesion. She grew very
close to her half brother and was able to take strength from a variety of
family relationships. However, her life required more effort in order to
find nurturance and support to enable her success. Compared to a child's
life who does not have to work so hard to assemble a support network,
Maya's life has been difficult.

MAGNIFIED CHALLENGES OF BLENDED FAMILIES

The desire to establish a blended family—much like the desire to marry—is
fueled by the various needs and motivations of the parents, such as
intimacy, companionship, and security, as well as social and public status. The social pressure of not wanting to be alone often nourishes this
desire. However, the challenges are often more daunting for those who
have been divorced and are still raising children.

In addition to those mentioned previously, the concerns can include

- differences in personality styles and temperaments of family
  members and various home dynamics
- expectations for manners and routines of both parents and
  children
- philosophies of both parents and children regarding the family
  and parenting roles, including faith practices (remember that
  children of divorce are often empowered by their parents'
  separation and establish premature independence and sense of
  control)
- health problems of individuals entering into the family
- loyalty conflicts, as reflected in Maya's story with her own mother
- unresolved court entanglements from prior relationships

It is important to recognize that the decision to divorce is rarely the wish of the children and may be a source of fear for them. According to the Divorce Study, 73 percent of children feared the breakup of their families. In the upheaval that comes from a parent's decision to form a new family by remarrying, children are forced to adjust, whether they are ready to or not. As a result, children learn to *not* express their genuine feelings through two mechanisms—by repression (internalizing feelings too painful for conscious awareness) and by suppression (not expressing thoughts and feelings). In the following example, both children have anger toward their fathers. The first child does *not* recognize the extent of her rage and fury at her father, referencing the feelings only as anger for his "distant behavior," and she seeks to banish him. The second child isn't in touch with her feelings toward her father at all and is instead focused exclusively on her mother.

Example of a *Repressed* Child's Response

I was very supportive of my mom, and angry at my father for his distant behavior. I saw over a pretty long period of time that there were irreconcilable differences, and I didn't want my parents to continue living as they did. There was no point pretending and playing house because our family life was nothing like it should have been. I hoped that once my parents were separated and divorced, my dad would find some measure of happiness and our relationship would change for the better.

—*Twenty-eight-year-old (age sixteen at the time of divorce)*

Example of a *Suppressed* Child's Response

I didn't want to make matters worse. I could see that my mother was hurting and that things were going horribly wrong. I was the strong one to be her shoulder to cry on, so my feelings didn't matter.

—*Sixteen-year-old (age eleven at the time of divorce)*

CHILDREN'S ADJUSTMENT TO
BLENDED FAMILIES

A child's history—meaning his or her personality, learned behaviors, and cultural background, as well as the relationships between the child and his or her parents—is a key factor for predicting his or her adjustment in a blended family.

Much as in the 1961 version of *The Parent Trap*, children often seek to restore the bond between their parents. Thus, the notion of a blended family represents the nail in the coffin of the parental marriage. One woman shared with me that even though she and her ex-husband had divorced, and though they had *each been remarried to other people for fifteen years*, her children continued to plot to have their parents reunite.

Research shows that children generally have a series of reactions to the concept of blended families, and that parents contemplating remarriage should consider these reactions.[2] We have already established that children need physical, emotional, and spiritual support to thrive, as well as love and recognition. When introducing a new spouse or siblings into the mix, consider that you are compounding the challenges that children already face as they develop. The following list illustrates some other behaviors exhibited by children (in particular age groups) worthy of consideration.

Children Under Age Ten

- Seek to elicit parental attention
- Are responsive to authority (adults)
- Have a need to align with their parents for affirmation and attention
- Require and are receptive to consistent support and guidance

Middle School Children and Young Adolescents
(Ages Eleven to Fourteen)

- Determine routines and role models
- May be resistant to or cautious of new family members
- Oppose imposed authority figures
- Withhold feelings and thoughts
- Decline affection and demonstrate apprehension

Adolescents (Mid to Late Teens)

- Separate from blended families and establish unique identities
- Disengage from blended-family activity
- Verbalize independence
- Seek alternative means of emotional support

Regarding the specific needs of young people, children desire to be understood in their relationships with new family members. Positive overtures and affection, and well-intended behaviors, are well received.

STRENGTHENING THE BLENDED FAMILY

To a large extent, nearly every recommendation that follows will enhance your family and your home. However, these recommendations are particularly important for blended families because these families are most vulnerable and require all the support available to them. I recommend that every family, including those families reforming following divorce, incorporates these suggestions.

1. Family Meetings

Regular gatherings where family members feel heard and respected can provide an opportunity to prevent a fire before a spark. During these meetings, upcoming activities, vacations, and special events can be planned. They also serve as opportunities to discuss concerns, problems, and strategies. Fair rules, listening skills, and respect for one another are imperatives for effective meetings. These meetings are not for parental sermons or lectures, or for the person with the loudest voice or largest pocketbook to dominate the conversation. Decisions should be made democratically—with equal involvement from both children and parents.

2. Family Meals

In today's world, researchers point to the lack of daily family meals as a source of instability in the home. Children often eat alone or without their parents.[3] Studies have shown that families who eat together, share daily experiences, and support laughter and play enjoy greater connections and deeper investment in the family.[4]

3. Family Tasks

A family is an organic unit, with each part contributing to the whole. The concept of family is founded on the belief that the whole is greater than the sum of its parts. When all family members contribute or participate in a task, such as preparing meals or preparing for a party, everyone is appreciated and recognized for his or her contributions and is able to feel like a crucial part of the family unit. This unit provides our identity, which has great meaning.

BLENDED FAMILY DILEMMAS

A common issue facing blended families is the perception of inequality. Have you ever heard your children express how unfairly they are treated in comparison to their stepsiblings or half sister or half brother? Here are three pain points to be aware of, as well as some practical advice on how to resolve them.

1. Lack of Preparedness

While a blended family is a family, it does not mean that parents act as parents and kids act as kids the same way they would in an intact home. Sometimes, one parent has never before been a parent, as in Maya's stepfather's situation. Other times, a stepfather or stepmother may not treat a child with the same type of love and respect he or she would dole out to his or her own biological child. In Maya's story, both her mother and her stepmother loved their children, but their own personal priorities had changed. This created confusion, sadness, and feelings of loss for their children. Yet this is not always a problem. Maya's stepmother emerged as a mentor to Maya because she was more attuned to Maya's inner workings, needs, and imagination than either of Maya's biological parents.

2. Rejection

Rejection of the child by the parent or stepparent is a problem that parents must seek to remedy. Parents may be tempted to dismiss that rejection as a function of adjustment, rather than zeroing in on the cause of the distress. Stepparents can be very helpful in addressing this conflict; however, mature stepparents recognize that they cannot assume authority or make their stepchildren accept them. They are largely placed in the unenviable position of having to win or earn the respect and acceptance of their stepchildren. This does not mean they should have to endure disrespect or abuse from resistant stepchildren or vice versa. Nevertheless, stepparents often have to manage resistance that may appear in the form of vengeful reactions, resentment, and sarcasm from their stepchildren. In the face of such behavior—as with most prudent parenting—positive, firm, and loving responses are usually the right course of action. However, patience on the stepparent's part is crucial.

3. Parent versus Stepparent

The term *stepparent* is awkward at best. As I mentioned previously, a stepparent is a *step* away from the real deal, or halfway there; yet a parent has a full-time commitment. He or she does not have half the privileges and responsibilities of raising children, but instead the entire duty. The step/half concept fosters inequity and could be considered a hurtful misnomer. The caveat for effective stepparenting requires that stepparents function more as supporters, counselors, or mentors, as the primary parent carries authority and disciplinary control over his or her children. The stepparent role is complex in that the investment does not necessarily equal a fair return. The best way to maintain control is to support authoritative parenting, as discussed in chapter 3, and not to overstep the biological parent's role. The perception of the stepparent as interloper will only create greater problems if he or she acts like an outsider, is not invested emotionally, and does not effectively balance his or her position in support of the spouse, the children's biological parent.

Belle's Story

Cynthia asked me to meet with both her and her teenage daughter, Belle, because Belle had become rebellious and sullen since Cynthia had gotten divorced and remarried. Once we met, there was no problem getting Belle to open up. She unleashed a litany of complaints about living with her new, blended family and her opposition to her stepfather, Bob.

Belle felt that her stepdad, a physician, did not approve of her or want her around. Crying, Belle blurted out, "You know what I feel, Mom? I'm less than a second-class citizen in my own home!"

Turning to me, Belle said, "When my mom married Bob, I went out the door! My mom does whatever is necessary to make him happy. She knows he doesn't like me. I sit at the dinner table, and it's as if I'm not even there. Even when his kids from his first marriage aren't there, they are the center of the conversation, and my mom plays along with it."

She continued, "When his kids come to the house, it's all excitement and celebration. If I'm home, it's an inconvenience for me to be around or an opportunity to find out what I'm wearing that he doesn't like or which of my friends don't meet his standards."

Belle was on a roll. "You want to talk, Mom? Well, let's do it! Admit that you throw me under the bus. You let him make his snide comments and pretend like I'm not even there, like I'm not even affected. Well, say something. You wanted this discussion. Here it is: I can't stand him and you love him—and he's smack in the middle of our so-called relationship. Do you get that?"

Cynthia was stunned. She was unsure how to respond to her daughter's comments. She stated that she loved Belle and wanted things to be better. After a few moments, she spoke about Belle's behaviors that most often provoked Bob. Given Cynthia's goals for meeting, I was surprised that she did not even try to create a method for constructively sorting out her daughter's pain and concerns. If she had invited Bob to counseling, the two of them could have spoken to Cynthia together to address the conflict in their relationship.

Belle made a strong case for the dangers of her mother's lack of parental oversight. Parents who divorce and remarry often make the mistake of assuming their new spouses and stepchildren will accept and welcome their children like in a harmonious episode of *The Brady Bunch*. But this assumption ignores feelings that all participants have repressed and suppressed. While new family adjustments may appear to work out just fine, more often there are issues that must be thoughtfully resolved before the situation can become truly amicable. Belle's fury is not unusual. In fact, Belle's response is even milder than what I have seen exhibited in other families who confronted their experiences of a stressful blend.

I was required to "look after" my stepsister because my mother worked and my stepfather was a shift worker. I did express my feelings about this arrangement with my mother by asking her, "How come I have to look after your problem?" Basically, I was told I had no choice; and I was not compensated for all that I did either, even though I felt I should have been.

—*Fifty-seven-year-old (age fifteen at the time of divorce)*

Introducing a new spouse and creating a blended family requires a great deal of preparation, empathy, and intervention. Parents can be effective by honoring their children's need for "space and place," allowing them to express their feelings, concerns, and wishes for their new family. Children need to be reassured and shown that the formation of a new family does not mean the termination of their established relationships with their birth parents, grandparents, aunts, uncles, cousins, and other important relatives.

Previous bonds should be maintained even as new families form, and children should not feel as though they are being forced into new family situations. One disturbing consequence may evolve: if parents do not make a concerted effort to help their children through this major change, they will find that they have sacrificed their children for their new lives.

Parental Recommendations

In blended families, children can feel as though their voices are unheard and that they have become a lower priority for their parents. Unless you address these changes, your children will struggle with their place and value in your new home and may resent the expectation that they should bond with their new family—often a family they had no say in creating.

The challenge of divorce requires children to adjust to the dismantling of their family as well as the formation of a new family or the absence of comforting family life. Divorce often dictates that children continue to adjust to an ever-growing network of new family members and relationships. As their parents remarry and establish blended families, children can find themselves lost in the shuffle. Newly blended families are not presented as an option to children—particularly minor children—but are often situations thrust on them. Children should not feel as though they are being forced into new family situations or forced on their new stepsiblings.

We zeroed in on the challenges both children and parents face in a blended family, keeping in mind that *all* families endure hurdles. Don't forget to be aware of your own motives and responses to all challenges. Avoid favoritism and make special personal time each day for every child. Whether you are a parent or stepparent, you are still a vital caregiver. Find support and address issues that concern you. Communicate with words and express loving intentions.

Nine Tips for Making Blended Families Work

Several stories have described parents leading lives with partners and even new stepchildren before the dust settled in a divorce, when children are still reeling from the adjustment. Working with your children and stepchildren's readiness for change will lead to a more successful adjustment of a blended family. By contrast, moving too quickly, without attending to unresolved feelings, is a strong predictor for rough sailing ahead.

1. *Attend to quality communication.* It is easier for everyone if the biological or primary parent leads communication with his or her child. While each partner has different strengths, it may appear easier for the more natural leader to take charge, or for the one who communicates more sensitively to guide exchanges. However, there is an inherent problem for stepparents who do not attend to emotional concerns regarding loss, authority, abandonment, and ownership—among several other related themes—which can easily get stirred when a non-parent imposes an unwelcome agenda or takes disciplinary action. Therefore, stepparents need to prepare themselves with thoughtful and sensitive strategies for meeting children's needs as the new family forms. A general rule of thumb is that the stepparent is the supportive counsel rather

than the lead parent, unless clearly engaged in that role by the parent and child. Therefore, it is wise to think through plans for communication and parenting before marrying.

2. *Give love a chance.* Don't expect to create the Brady Bunch or an idyllic family overnight. Real relationships, as you know from your past, take time and work. Your enthusiasm for your spouse will not necessarily transfer to his or her children. Learn who they are and try to understand the children's uncertainties, resistance, and confusion—which may not be rational or have anything to do with you.

3. *Respect boundaries.* Children are often "imported" into adult relationships with expectations that they will align with a new order. They may genuinely not like the arrangement of people, personalities, or accommodations—and they're entitled to their opinions. Children may feel mixed loyalties about getting settled without their other parent, with images and visions of their siblings or the other parent who is not participating in your home or event, and have a hollow feeling about the new home.

4. *Act positively and honestly.* Your actions will be most effective when they are attentive and constructive. However, children's hurt feelings may lead them on a mission to unravel your dream, as does an unruly class with a well-meaning substitute teacher. Set limits, and be prepared for those limits to be challenged.

5. *Set reasonable expectations.* Because kids—particularly those over seven—are not "just kids" in position to take instructions, you will want to set your expectations with your spouse and reevaluate your plans to be sure that they are realistic. You may even want to invite the children in the planning, without imposing too many requests—especially when designing a home that they may not necessarily be interested in supporting. Include their ideas to enable them to feel as though they can buy in to this plan and that they have a legitimate role and voice.

6. *Focus on self-control.* Without feeling guilty or defensive, think

about your next move, what you can do, and how you can manage your thoughts, feelings, and actions. Externalizing problems in relationship to others is a design for failure and difficulties.

7. *Identify and acknowledge your needs and feelings.* While you will not want to become pals with your stepchildren or blur the boundaries of your role with your children and stepchildren, you want to be in touch with your experiences. Your partner needs to understand your experiences. It is important that you do not deny or suppress your feelings, as this will only generate distress and resentment. If you need help, ask for it and arrange to get it.

8. *Define your role.* Just as there are all kinds of parents and kids, there are all kinds of stepparents. How do you understand your role in this family? What would you like to see occur? What problems do you envision as significant, and what do you think you can bring to each of the children?

9. *Be yourself.* You bring unique gifts to this family and potentially to each of the children in your home. Do not try to be something you are not. Through a sound self-assessment, you will know if you are freely and spontaneously engaged and modeling qualities of healthy freedom needed by the children in your blended family.

In chapter 9, we will discuss how the heart emerges as the most powerful tool you possess to preserve and enjoy your children—the life-saver for the family encountering the whirlwind of divorce. By engaging it properly, you form a robust bond between you and your family.

Chapter 9

PRESERVE LOVING RELATIONSHIPS

We chose to live very close by each other when we got divorced, so the kids always could run from one house to another. We got to be friends and co-parents after the divorce, and we often get together for a cup of coffee, to ensure that we have the same parenting strategy. That makes the children feel safe, and it shows them that divorce isn't the end of the world, as long as you make the conscious decision to cooperate and work together toward improving not only the kids' lives but also your own.

—PARENT (MARRIED SIX YEARS)

___

Parental Oversight 9

Loss of the experience of love is the most common and agonizing drawback that children of divorce report. By providing love and empowering your children to access sources that sustain and strengthen their love throughout life, you will successfully counter this negative consequence of divorce.

> It was all about them—we would go to see my dad and listen to tirades about how loyal we were to her. Then he would take his second wife and son, who went to a private school and lived in a

beautiful home, on fabulous trips. We lived in rental homes until we finally moved into a housing project when I was in junior high. We should have all been in counseling. It has affected my sisters and me for fifty-four years. So sad.

—Sixty-year-old (age six at the time of divorce)

[My parents] were off doing their own thing. My dad was really torn up because my mom left him for another man. He was sad; and my mom acted like she did nothing [wrong]. She just went on with her life like she was finally free. It was so sad; and it tears me up thinking about it to this day. The pain is so deep. My inner child will never get over it. As an adult, I see that it had to happen. I just don't think they did everything they could to work through their issues. They just gave up. My mom literally moved on and got pregnant and remarried within a month of being divorced.

—Thirty-four-year-old (age eleven at the time of divorce)

My mother made me her confidante when I was fifteen. She shared with me every detail of my father's affair. She went into a deep depression; and I knew that I not only lost my father, but also my mother. I now only have a friend's relationship with my mother. I mourn the mom I once had—even now at thirty-eight years old.

—Thirty-eight-year-old (age fifteen at the time of divorce)

When forty-eight-year-old Sarah came to see me, she was unsure of what was really disturbing her. She had a fulfilling career, a beautiful family, and a twenty-three-year marriage to a man whom she loved deeply. It wasn't until we spoke about her childhood that we touched on what was troubling her. Sarah confessed she had never overcome her sorrow over her parents' divorce.

"I never knew my parents were unhappy," she said. "My parents didn't share their emotions with us prior to the divorce. My sister, my brother, and I were still in middle school when they simply announced one night after dinner that 'It was best for the family' to get a divorce. Then they said that we would live with our mom and visit our dad."

Sarah explained that she and her siblings were devastated, but they couldn't share their feelings because there was no space to do that: "It was all about them—their needs, their decision, their lives. We simply had to go along with the plan. No one ever asked if we liked it. Our feelings didn't matter. Neither of them asked how we felt, nor did they say they were sorry for disrupting our lives."

Years later, Sarah tried to discuss the divorce and its impact on her with her mother, but her mother replied, "You have your own life to live. Why stir up unpleasant issues from the past?"

Sarah didn't dare bring the subject up with her father until she was thirty-two. When she asked him if he'd been having an affair prior to the divorce, his only response was, "It was a different world in the 1970s. Everyone slept around." She then asked him how he could have done that to his family.

"He couldn't admit to his self-serving behaviors and sneakiness, or even express guilt or remorse," Sarah told me. "He said he kept these two worlds separate—not recognizing that this was tormenting me or that I had a stake in the matter."

Sarah wasn't alone in her suffering. Her sister became a cutter, injuring herself in an attempt to deal with her emotional pain. Her brother abused drugs and was involved in several car accidents. Her parents never acknowledged that their own issues might be related to the family's breakup.

Sarah said she felt that her parents' lack of concern for their children's feelings was a form of torture. As a result, she said she felt as if she were "emotionally frozen in time."

"I don't think they want to see the instability and misery that they created for us by shifting us around like luggage every week between homes and by coming up with rules for us to follow rather than asking us who we were and what we were feeling," she said.

Sarah still yearned to confront her parents with the fact that they failed their children by forcing them to suppress their emotions and feelings. "I want to tell them they screwed up big time, and that I'm getting to be an old lady and still feel it!"

Sarah's story exemplifies how the breakdown of loving relationships carries long-term effects. Adults frequently see me for counseling still deeply wounded even decades following the divorces that broke up their families. They have often experienced failed relationships and divorce themselves because of unresolved hurt, anger, and insecurities related to their parents' divorces.

Divorced parents retain responsibility for helping their kids understand and process the impact of the breakup on their emotional lives, even when these children become adults. In this way, children of divorce can understand themselves and build healthy and lasting relationships going forward.

Divorced parents may be tired of talking about the uncomfortable realities of the past. But a more appropriate response is to take responsibility for the collateral damage they've caused and actively guard against the breakdown of the loving parent-child bond so that their children are not left burdened and wounded.

The lack of explanation made me feel like life was very unpredictable and anything could happen at any time. Also, I don't remember my father ever saying "I miss you" or "I still love you even though I'm not here much" or anything like that. As an adult, I realize that he is emotionally barren in general. But as a little kid, I thought that we were somehow defective, and so he threw us away.

—*Forty-four-year-old (age three and a half at the time of divorce)*

I think I've become more isolated. I've gotten to where I sleep a lot more because I constantly feel emotionally drained. I started doing stupid things because I feared opening up to anyone. I've probably gotten to a point where I don't necessarily feel suicidal, but I wouldn't care if anything bad happened to me. I've felt abandoned. I've felt not good enough. I have felt like a burden and a disappointment.

—Seventeen-year-old (age eleven at the time of divorce)

The Single Most Important Gift in Parenting

The late psychologist and author Judith Wallerstein conducted a pioneering study that followed a group of children of divorce from the 1970s through the 1990s. She interviewed the children at eighteen months, and at five-, ten-, fifteen-, and twenty-five-year intervals. She expected to find that, over time, they had recovered from the emotional trauma of divorce. Instead, she discovered that these children of divorce still experienced fear of failure, loss, change, and conflict.[1]

Divorce can have lasting consequences on your children's development and the ways they navigate their lives. Your bond with your children is the most significant factor in determining how they cope with your divorce. Consider the following questions:

- Do you expect that your children will be resilient to the impact the divorce will have in their lives? Do you tell them to "toughen up" or deflect their questions and simply say, "You have to grow up and deal"?
- How are you mending the negative toll that divorce has had on your children?
- How do you build the best connections with your children to counter the damage and consequences of divorce?
- Can your children feel your love and count on you?

I am a divorced mother of two children. Even though my husband and I chose not to be married any longer, we still remain allies for our two children. I wish someone would have done this for me. I would be a different person today if [my parents] had. To this day, I feel so divided by their divorce. My goal is to make sure my children never feel a strain from our divorce. This should be the norm for divorced parents. I am really proud of what we have been able to accomplish, and our children are better for it.

—*Twenty-eight-year-old (age seven at the time of divorce)*

I had always had a very close bond with my children, but it's gotten even closer. It's hard for children to realize that their parents suffer from the same human frailties as the rest of the world, but it's also strengthening when you discover together how resilient you can be in the face of tragic events.

—*Parent (married twenty-five years)*

Children find meaning in their attachments and connections stemming from the quality care we provide for them. Keep in mind that the way we experience love forms our map for loving. Therefore, our children learn how to love from how we love and loved them.

By contrast, divorce confirms the dissolution of a parental union and often ushers in a period of instability and complications in the parent-child relationship. Children must handle these changes as they yearn to retain their own personal connections with each parent individually. **The single most important gift all parents must provide for their children in the face of divorce is love—a powerful antidote to the potentially destructive chain of events caused by divorce.** Though divorce fractures the example children see of love between their parents, this does not mean that the need for love and nurturance—essential elements for a child's healthy development—terminates or ceases to grow.

I grew up overcompensating because of a fear of failure. I lack the ability to communicate my emotions and my feelings. I am not so good socially. I shut people out.

—*Fifty-year-old (age six at the time of divorce)*

I no longer had my ethnic identity (Scandinavian) as my new step-mother was American, and my new life revolved totally around her and what was best for her. I didn't have my mother in my life until my twenties; and then because she was in it at that point, my father removed himself from my life. So in a nutshell, as a child I grieved for my mother. As an adult, I grieved for my father.

—Fifty-year-old (age five at the time of divorce)

When love is absent or insufficient, children face a poor prognosis in both the short and long term (as described in chapter 1). But children of divorce are not condemned to being shut out of love unless both parents abdicate their primary responsibility to care and provide for their children. Without that care and attention, children face many obstacles, as they are left without a map or a living guide, leaving them uncertain before crossroads and potential dead ends. The good news is that when one or both parents protect their love for their children, the prognosis is much more optimistic. When they receive genuine love and support, children will

- develop a healthy identity;
- demonstrate confidence in relating with others;
- give and receive freely in relationships;
- learn about boundaries and comfort in intimacy;
- show resilience in managing the expected and unexpected in relationships and throughout their life journeys; and
- have an awareness and capacity to love and be loved.

I think when you know better, you do better. I realized one day that I never came with an owner's manual—nor did life. So, I cut [my parents] a break for the mistakes they made; and I continued to learn how I can make the impact that I want to make and how to be responsible for what happens to me.

—Thirty-nine-year-old (age five at the time of divorce)

My mother is currently on her third marriage and still a very un-happy and lost soul. My father got clean years ago and has made great strides to improve himself. I can say they each showed me how to be and how not to be as I grew up. Dealing with their abuse and watching their failures, I felt very strongly about having self-awareness and not making similar mistakes. I have done pre-marriage counseling, marriage counseling, and personal therapy through the years to learn to deal with my issues and try to be the best person, spouse, and hopefully someday mother I can be.

—*Thirty-two-year-old (age ten at the time of divorce)*

The essential love that you impart to your children equips them with these four discernible capacities:

1. *The ability to know and love oneself.* Children learn to love them-selves through their relationships with their parents, who serve as the initial and primary contact to experientially define how to love and to understand their self-worth. Their first relationship is the blueprint for all those that follow. A proper understanding of love for parents, however, is dependent on knowing what love is and how best to nurture it.

2. *The ability to confidently relate to others.* Your love is a posi-tive affirmation of your children's importance in your life and helps them develop a positive sense of self. Your children return this gift through their bond with you and in other significant relationships. They love you back, and they feel secure in their attachment to you. This dynamic evolves as your engagement with your children deepens.

   Note that you must nurture the whole child. If you validate your children based solely on their athletic performances, aca-demic performances, or appearances, they will not see themselves as being loved as a whole individual. Rather, they will feel as though only parts of themselves—largely superficial—are worthy of love. Children who are only praised for one aspect of their personalities or talents are left feeling insecure and unsure about themselves, but you can deepen their sense of self by loving them for who they are, not for what they can do.

Because of the pressure of divorce, parents may fail to recognize and nurture the uniqueness of their children. When you understand this, it is not difficult to see why children may seek attention and validation outside of the home, even from people who do not have their best interests in mind. Therefore, you are in the most critical position to fulfill this need that your children have during this challenging time.

3. *The ability to maintain healthy boundaries and intimacy.* In divorce, examples of these abilities often fall away and create uncertainty about a child's capacity to establish and maintain ongoing relationships. Psychologists say that relationships replace relationships. By constructively working through, discussing, and understanding the difficulties in your marital relationship and providing healthy models for strengthening relationships, your children will distinguish the kinds of relationships they need and those that they need to refine.

4. *The ability to demonstrate resilience as relationships change and grow.* Divorce often tests the limits of one's resilience and capacities. By focusing your attention on nurturing your children, and by developing your resolve to do what is right, you are teaching your children to do the same. Your children's ability to confront obstacles and persevere will be strengthened from watching you. By remaining engaged in loving actions, divorced parents can model behavior for their children.

At one point during my divorce, my seven-year-old was embarrassed that her friends at school might learn that my wife and I were divorcing. One little boy passed a note behind my daughter's back, making a large letter "D" with an arrow pointing to her, revealing that "Ariana's parents were divorced." Ariana was understandably distressed. After reporting the details, she told me that she did not want me to resolve the matter by speaking with the boy or her teacher—which wasn't my intention. However, I told her that we should never be afraid of the truth or avoid managing problems. Instead, we need to respond honestly and directly.

Following our conversation, Ariana and I agreed that I would call the boy's parents, as I did not think that the little boy understood how disturbing his actions were for her. I thought this might be an opportunity to help him grow as well. When calling the boy's mother, I stated that I did not believe her son had intended to hurt Ariana's feelings, but that he had. The mother responded very sensitively. The boy apologized to Ariana, ending the anxiety and unnecessary strain she felt.

Protecting your children requires attending constructively to difficulties they experience, even if they appear insignificant. Children need to be able to count on their parents with small issues to help them manage the large ones. A demonstration of love by coming through for them is infinitely more powerful than only talking about it.

Certainly, this relatively small matter could have created even more complexity. But that is no reason to shy away from addressing an incident. Even if things get worse, there is always an opportunity to learn from a situation—if you have confirmed for yourself that your heart and mind are driven by positive and constructive motives. Moreover, the chance for you to come through for your children, to empower them when they are distraught, and to convey that their distress is worthy of your time and attention is priceless.

On the positive side, I married a wonderful man a year later who bonded with [my child] almost immediately and had her as a top priority, so by getting divorced I was able to get training for a career, marry for love, and have a stable home life. On the negative side, since I had to give my ex full custody to get myself where I could take care of her, he ruined his relationship with her (he allowed his parental tasks to be taken over by his mother, never did get a job, and to this day is on welfare). She lost her bond with him during the time she stayed with him. I had to fight to get her back, but I did and found out that I in fact rescued her from some things I thought would never have happened but did.

—Parent (married five years)

While most parents seek to establish lifelong bonds with their sons and daughters, they often do not recognize that there's no time like the present—even during a divorce—to be *present* for their children. I cannot emphasize enough that *now is the time* for coming through with love. There is prophetic truth in the classic song "Cat's in the Cradle" by Harry Chapin. In the little boy's refrain, he longs for his father to come home, repeatedly asking throughout his childhood when it will happen. The father promises that he will, yet time passes through many more critically "missed moments." Finally, the retired father extends himself as ready to get together, but the son, now grown, learned well from his model, saying that he promises he will but can't right now. The son has internalized the same kind of love he was taught.

The song gives credence to the maxim that "what goes around, comes around." When parents do not demonstrate loving relationships with their children, both bonds of the relationship are frayed, the children suffer and so ultimately the parents, and opportunities are lost. What follows is heartbreak as parents realize that there's no going back in time to repair the lost relationship.

PARENTAL RECOMMENDATIONS

It is abundantly clear that continuing to model love in the shadow of divorce is critical for raising stable and emotionally healthy children who will become stable and emotionally healthy adults. But what exactly does that look like?

If you heed the recommendations of previous chapters—be attuned to your kids, nurture them, provide stability for them, and preserve their sense of trust—you will be well on your way. But there are two additional considerations I want to impart.

1. *Love as a sacred connection.* First, I believe that the essence of loving is born out of something larger than us, as memorialized in the great spiritual traditions of the world. Loving is a sacred connection: the highest human function, entrusted to us by God. It is a process toward oneness, union, and connectedness.

    The faith traditions are imbued with the energy for spiritual union that is essential to our nature, and are confirmed today as essential for health and well-being through science. Buddhism teaches that compassion is the way the suffering ends and that compassion is required for the goal of enlightenment. Christianity emphasizes sacrificial love (to love God with all your heart, soul, mind, and strength, and to love your neighbor as yourself) as the critical connection for both life on this earth and life eternal. Islam teaches that you will not enter paradise until you believe, and you will not believe until you love. Hinduism emphasizes *prema*, a required sacrament to relinquish selfishness; only love accesses the part of us that is like the soul. In Judaism, steadfast kindness is celebrated in the community, especially the family, as an essential ingredient of love.

    While your marriage may have been a wonderful laboratory where your children could learn how to love, your divorce may show them how *not* to love—or inadvertently teach them that love does not exist. Your spiritual resources can provide a critical antidote to the toxicity of this experience and realign you with the strength you need for your heart and the hearts of the children who depend on you.

Unconditional love—the kind of love we must have for our children—is a love that calls us to go beyond ourselves, as in the model of *agape* love demonstrated by Jesus Christ. The chaos of divorce may cause your children to act out in ways that lead you to question whether you feel *agape* love for them. It may even be tempting to figuratively or literally cast them out, using Matthew 5:30 as justification ("If your right hand causes you to sin, cut it off and cast it from you; for it is more profitable for you that one of your members perish, than for your whole body to be cast into hell"). But recall that Jesus also said, "Father, forgive them, for they do not know what they do" (Luke 23:34). Unconditional love leads us to enter into our children's conflicts, to stand above their reactions, and to take a course of action that does not lead us to cut them off but rather maintains an open door.

2. *Love takes numerous forms.* Gary Chapman struck an international chord in his book *The Five Love Languages: How to Express Heartfelt Commitment to Your Mate* as he explained that people understand and express love in different ways. Although his book describes five forms of love, there are countless more.[2] Marital problems often stem from a lack of understanding of and communication about the ways each partner loves and is loved. Additionally, it's important to recognize that our own notions of love continue to evolve, as will our children's. So while we may have a heartfelt need to love and to be loved in a particular way, we must be aware that our kids may require a different kind of love entirely.

The advice given throughout this book builds to this point: loving each of our children as a unique human being is the single greatest step we can take toward minimizing the harm that comes to them through divorce. Listening and responding to their unique fears and concerns; building bonds with them over their specific interests and passions; protecting them from what they do not need to know and including them in what they do, based on their particular circumstances—these are all ways of showing our children that they are important to us, that they matter, and that we will not allow them to become collateral damage.

A FINAL WORD

Redirecting Your Divorce
Through Spiritual Life

Faced with divorce, a family's life voyage slams headfirst into an iceberg, and the potential fate of its members is demise. Tossed into parts, family members may become engulfed in waves of destructive forces. Is there a captain of our ship? Are all passengers accounted for? How do we or will we survive?

Regardless of a family's past or present religious affiliation, faith is a powerful resource for wading through the storm of divorce. Faith supports stabilization and direction, enabling each member to navigate a course that supports personal, emotional, spiritual, and physical potential.

The capacity to give and receive freely in relationships emerges from the critical connections one forms with God, self, and others. Spiritual contact is essential for restoring ourselves and responding to others, particularly in the challenges of a crisis such as divorce. Our critical connections provide a model for how our love grows, based on our evolving development in our relationships with others and with God. God inspires us to confront our limits and restores us, leading us beyond our capabilities and toward our potential so that we can experience love through greater understanding, virtue, care, and sacrifice. Through spiritual contact, we are fueled to grow, to give, to evolve, and to initiate. We move beyond our personal limitations toward new heights by gaining perspective through our spiritual nature and connection. We are able to see more clearly by giving and receiving with ourselves, and with others, in view of a higher purpose. I believe that we are all children of God, regardless of our roles on this earth. I also believe that God—not the individual—is the source of love that informs our love for one another, and that parents are trusted by God to care for their children. To love well, we must draw on our source of the greatest, highest love—that which infuses us with the ability to provide spiritual and loving nurturance and guidance to our children.

As divorce depletes parental energies, it makes sense that in order to maintain a reservoir of energy for ourselves and for our children, we must be restored and tap into this spiritual energy available to us. By engaging in a process of prayer, inspiration, or communication with our spiritual core, we are infused with an energy that will both deepen and develop the sense of love expressed through our critical connections. **Power and energy that we do not possess on our own can work through us when we tap into the Spirit.**

When I interviewed Maya Angelou, she shared with me how the meaning of faith and her relationship with God empowered her to persevere. She described her challenges and how prayer expanded her vision of life. During our conversation, she sang a church hymn for me that encapsulated this message and her process. "Lord, Don't Move the Mountain" encourages us to open our eyes beyond our wants—despite our temporal pain—so that we can discover the power of a living faith. The lyrics ask not for obstacles to be removed from our paths but that we be given the strength we need to overcome them. (You can go to YouTube to hear a moving Mahalia Jackson performance of this piece. It's well worth a listen.)[1]

After Maya sang, she wiped her brow. After pausing for a few moments, she looked at me with tear-filled eyes, holding her hands together, and said, "That's some deep stuff!"

We cannot always choose our challenges, but we can choose how we manage them. Through an authentic spiritual life, parents can model how living actions of faith can guide them and their children to do what is right. During my divorce, my children and I retained an active prayer life and found that this critical connection gave us strength and direction. This experience deepened our relationships with God, which was a personal resource for each family member. As we read the Bible together or participated in prayer, the God-presence that we felt was palpable. Confusion gave way to vivid direction and clarity. When considering whatever difficulty we were facing, once again I would say, "Do your best and leave the rest to God." I never thought this path was vacant or ineffective; instead I knew it was real and believe it led to responsiveness and wisdom.

An awareness and capacity to love and be loved is the most important task in parenting. Here, again, the critical connections inform the ways in which parents can most effectively express their love for their children. Spiritual guidance can instruct both children and parents about loving behaviors as well as how to express and share that love. Parents should not feel the need to make up for a divorce by showering their children with gifts. Nor should parents allow children to exploit their efforts in order to win support during the divorce struggle. By serving as an example of engagement in spiritual life, you as a parent set a higher bar for life that guides all of your relationships. This ultimately leads children to establish their own spiritual connections for guidance and support.

Though we were shocked by the unexpected calamity of divorce in our home, our connection to and trust in the higher power of God provided support and direction in this time of isolation and fear. When my children learned that my former wife and I were headed for a divorce, it shook each of them to his or her core. It was customary for my family to pray together before meals and in our home. Saying a prayer—even in an awkward moment of uncertainty—brought us peace and unity. I supported my children to secure their bond with God because I knew that the waters ahead would be rough, and each of our decisions would draw on our alignment with him to restore and secure our family.

My own view as a parent has been that God entrusts us with the greatest blessing of all: giving us an opportunity to participate in the creation of life and guide our children to achieve their potential. Even when divorce perpetuates some of the harshest and worst feelings imaginable, faith and spiritual power can provide direction for what is good, true, and right. I believe that a relationship with God reinforces our values of respect, honor, and love—essential aspects of all healthy relationships—that become unrecognizable when parents may be thrashing about in divorce.

Parents need to take control of rightful actions for themselves and their children. Spirituality sustains us by providing access to greater guidance in faith, which fortifies us and drives us to undertake life's challenges with solid values, direction, and identity. Even if forces beyond your control change your family unit, you must remain focused on the sustenance of vital relationships (especially between you and your children), which can be nurtured through personal experience with a powerful God.

Trusting experiences are essential for strong relationships with oneself, others, and one's spiritual truth. When parents do not offer a single voice or message to their children during divorce, children can turn to their spiritual beliefs as a powerful resource and a reminder that they are not alone. They may discover the real dependency on something they can always count on—the healthy dependency that is much greater than dependency on one's self. My children wanted to pray together regularly during the divorce; they felt that this gathering with God was a clear symbol of us assembling together and not being alone. God will not fail you. Your spiritual foundation can deepen your critical connections, secure your values, guide your actions and direction, and fortify you to meet life's challenges.

Our spirituality empowers us, showing us how to love. When we live in faith, our fears, anger, despair, and confusion are transformed through trust, understanding, and love.

APPENDIX

The Divorce Study Survey

1. PARTICIPANTS

The target population for the Divorce Study was divorced parents with children assessed through the Parents' Survey as well as children of divorce assessed through the Children's Survey. There were more than ten thousand total responses to both surveys. Participants were predominately from the United States.

2. METHODOLOGICAL APPROACH

In 2010, two surveys were designed with the goal of understanding the experiences of children and parents who have gone through divorce. Both surveys were placed on the website of the *Dr. Phil* television show—one survey for parents with children of divorce and the other for children of divorce (see surveys below). Data was collected over a five-year period. Researchers at Harvard University analyzed the surveys, which were collected through the online service SurveyMonkey. There were more than 10,000 respondents, which included approximately 4,300 child respondents and 5,700 parent respondents. The results of those surveys provided the findings presented in *Collateral Damage*. The results of the responses from the Children's Survey were represented by the following demographic categories: age when children learned their parents would divorce, current age, and information about the divorce. Results from the responses of the Parents' Survey were represented by the following demographic categories: length of time married before the divorce, length of the divorce process, years since the divorce, and which parent initiated the divorce. Participants were treated in accordance with the American Psychological Association's Ethical Principles of Psychologists and Code of Conduct, including 2010 Amendments.

3. ANALYSIS

Most of the questions in the survey elicited qualitative, or descriptive, answers from the participants. To convert qualitative responses into quantitative or measurable data, machine learning techniques were implemented with Python programming language. Survey responses from each of the respondents were then classified into particular categories. Microsoft SQL Server was employed as the database management software, and Microsoft Excel was used to report the findings.

4. THE DIVORCE STUDY SURVEYS AND RESULTS

Below are both the Parents' and Children's Surveys. The percentages reveal how all respondents answered their respective survey questions.

Parents' Survey

Quantitative Results

1. Did you seek the divorce or did your spouse?

I sought to divorce	**61%**
Spouse	**24%**
Both	**15%**

2. How would you characterize your divorce (select the answer that best describes your situation)?

   Mild, by mutual agreement:

"We just grew apart."	**7%**

   Undesirable, but necessary:

"We weren't on the same course."	**24%**

   Disruptive and unexpected:

"I never imagined this."	**24%**

   Volatile and polemic:

"Highly contentious."	**19%**

   Explosive and destructive:

"A nightmare—terror."	**26%**

3. In the end, would you want to divorce this person again—given the process and aftermath of the divorce process?

Yes	**79%**
No	**21%**

4. Did you discuss the plan to divorce with your children?

Yes	**49%**
No	**51%**

5. Did you feel you adequately discussed your children's feelings about the divorce?

Yes	**51%**
No	**49%**

6. Did you postpone your divorce because of your children?

Yes	**38%**
No	**62%**

7. Did your children have a voice in the decision of your divorce?

Yes	**12%**
No	**88%**

8. Did the children try to prevent the divorce?

Yes	**14%**
No	**86%**

9. Did you feel equipped to respond to your children's needs in the throes of the divorce?

Yes	**55%**
No	**45%**

10. Did you draw on professional help to assist the children with their adjustment?

Yes	**56%**
No	**44%**

11. Do you think that your relationship with your children improved or suffered as a result of your divorce?

Improved	**47%**
Suffered	**31%**
Not sure	**22%**

12. Do you feel regrets for the impact of your divorce on your children?

Yes	**72%**
No	**28%**

Qualitative Results Converted to Quantitative Results

13. How did you factor in your children in your decision to divorce?

No: not at all	**22%**
No: wanted to but child was too small to understand	**3%**
Yes: very little	**6%**
Yes: partially	**45%**
Yes: throughout	**14%**

14. How did your children respond to news of the divorce?

Pleased	**9%**
Normal/not sure	**27%**
Disappointed and sad	**25%**
Extremely disappointed and scared	**39%**

15. What were the impacts of your divorce on your children's life?

Positive	**6%**
No effect	**10%**
Negative	**84%**

16. What were the long-term effects of the divorce for the children?

Positive	**5%**
No effect	**15%**
Negative	**80%**

17. Did life improve for the kids following divorce?

Yes	**48%**
Yes, only slightly	**5%**
No	**7%**
No, got worse	**40%**

Children's Survey

Quantitative Results

1. Who told you?

Mother	**47%**
Father	**11%**
Both	**24%**
Other	**18%**

2. Did you speak to your parents about your feelings?

Yes	**31%**
No	**69%**

3. Do you think that you were the cause of the divorce?

Yes	**18%**
No	**82%**

4. Did you feel that you were in the middle of your parents' divorce (e.g., custody battle, visitation decisions, and legal matters)?

Yes	**57%**
No	**43%**

5. Did you have a therapist help you with your feelings when the divorce occurred?

Yes	**18%**
No	**82%**

6. If you had a therapist, was the therapist helpful?

Yes	**33%**
No	**67%**

7. Do you feel that your parents did a good job managing the impact of the divorce for you?

Yes	**28%**
No	**72%**

Qualitative Results Converted to Quantitative Results

8. How did you feel when you learned that your parents would divorce?

Pleased/happy	**21%**
Normal/understood	**14%**
Sad and disappointed	**65%**

9. If you spoke to your parents about your family's divorce, what did you express? If you did not express your feelings to your parents, why not?

Did not express anything	**80%**
Expressed understanding/support	**3%**
Expressed disappointment/sadness	**17%**

10. What were your greatest fears about the divorce?

No fears	**19%**
Family break	**73%**
Which side to choose: mother or father	**8%**

11. What did your parents do that helped you most through the divorce process?

No real involvement with the divorce process	**4%**
Counseling and keeping in touch	**39%**
Nothing much	**57%**

12. What did your parents do that hurt you most or made managing the divorce difficult?

Nothing significant	**5%**
No care or involvement in the divorce process	**38%**
Choice of parents	**5%**
Verbal or physical abuse	**52%**

13. Who was the most helpful person to you during your parents' divorce?

Parents	**22%**
Siblings and friends	**20%**
Relatives (including Steps)	**30%**
Others	**4%**
No one	**24%**

14. How did the divorce affect your life?

Negatively	**76%**
No effect	**1%**
Positively	**13%**

NOTES

Chapter 1: Attune to Your Child

1. Graham Music, *Nurturing Natures: Attachment and Children's Emotional, Sociocultural and Brain Development* (New York: Psychology Press, 2010).
2. Emily J. Escott, "Neurocognitive Functioning in Children with Histories of Early Deprivation, Change in Caregiver, and Other Stressors" (PhD diss., Adler School of Professional Psychology, 2014), 6.
3. Arnold J. Sameroff and Katherine L. Rosenblum, "Psychosocial Constraints on the Development of Resilience," *Annals of the New York Academy of Sciences* 1094, no. 1 (2006): 119.
4. Jay D. Teachman, "Childhood Living Arrangements and the Intergenerational Transmission of Divorce," *Journal of Marriage and the Family* 64 (2002): 722.
5. Taina Huurre, Hanna Junkkari, and Hillevi Aro, "Long-term Psychosocial Effects of Parental Divorce," *European Archives of Psychiatry and Clinical Neuroscience* 256, no. 4 (2006): 260.
6. Daniel Potter, "Psychosocial Well-Being and the Relationship Between Divorce and Children's Academic Achievement," *Journal of Marriage and Family* 72 (2010): 934.
7. Huurre, Junkkari, and Aro, "Long-term Psychosocial Effects of Parental Divorce," 261, 26.
8. Take, for example, the first verse of rapper Eminem's "Sing for the Moment," which depicts a young man's behavior after his dad has walked out on him. Eminem, vocal performance of "Sing for the Moment," by Marshall Mathers, Jeff Bass, Luis Resto, Steve King, and Steven Tyler, recorded 2000–2001, on *The Eminem Show* (Aftermath Entertainment /Shady Records/Interscope Records, 2003), compact disc.

9. Teachman, "Childhood Living Arrangements and the Intergenerational Transmission of Divorce," *Journal of Marriage and the Family* 64 (2002): 722.

10. David S. DeGarmo and Marion S. Forgatch, "Early Development of Delinquency Within Divorced Families: Evaluating a Randomized Preventative Intervention Trial," *Developmental Science* 8, no. 3 (2005): 230.

11. Leslie Gordon Simons and Rand D. Conger, "Linking Mother–Father Differences in Parenting to a Typology of Family Parenting Styles and Adolescent Outcomes," *Journal of Family Issues* 28, no. 2 (2007): 213.

12. Clorinda E. Velez et al., "Protecting Children from the Consequences of Divorce: A Longitudinal Study of the Effects of Parenting on Children's Coping Processes," *Child Development* 82, no. 1 (2011): 245.

13. Huurre, Junkkari, and Aro, "Long-Term Psychosocial Effects of Parental Divorce," 261.

14. Jennifer E. Lansford, "Parental Divorce and Children's Adjustment," *Perspectives on Psychological Science* 4, no. 2 (2009): 142–43.

15. J. T. Chirban, *Spirituality in Client Care: The Role of Faith, Meditation, and Mindfulness in Healing* (Nashville: Cross Country Education, 2014), 53.

16. E. Mark Cummings et al., "Interparental Discord and Child Adjustment: Prospective Investigations of Emotional Security as an Explanatory Mechanism," *Child Development* 77, no. 1 (2006): 133.

17. Ibid., 137.

Chapter 2: Manage Emotions and Stormy Situations

1. John Mordechai Gottman, *What Predicts Divorce? The Relationship Between Marital Processes and Marital Outcomes* (New York: Psychology Press, 2014), 158–80.

2. Robert Emery, *The Truth About Children and Divorce: Dealing with the Emotions So You and Your Children Can Thrive* (New York: Plume, 2006).

3. Mark A. Whisman and Lisa A. Uebelacker, "Impairment and Distress Associated with Relationship Discord in a National Sample of Married or Cohabiting Adults," *Journal of Family Psychology* 20, no. 3 (2006): 369.

4. E. Mark Cummings and Patrick T. Davies, *Marital Conflict and Children: An Emotional Security Perspective* (New York: Guilford Press, 2011), 133.

5. Cummings, et al., "Interparental Discord and Child Adjustment."

6. Maxim quoted in Ben Carson, *Think Big: Unleashing Your Potential for Excellence* (Grand Rapids: Zondervan, 1996), 255.
7. Kate Kelland, "One in 12 Teenagers Self Harm, Study Finds," *Reuters*, November 17, 2011, http://www.reuters.com/article /us-self-harm-idUSTRE7AG02520111117.
8. James Gorman, "Scientists Hint at Why Laughter Feels So Good," *New York Times*, September 13, 2011, http://www.nytimes.com/2011/09/14 /science/14laughter.html?_r=0.
9. Kathleen Doheny, "Why We Cry: The Truth About Tearing Up," WebMD. com, October 30, 2009, http://www.webmd.com/balance/features /why-we-cry-the-truth-about-tearing-up.
10. J. A. Astin, "Stress Reduction Through Mindfulness Meditation," *Psychotherapy and Psychosomatics* 66.2 (1997): 97–106.
11. Søren Kierkegaard, *Purity of Heart Is to Will One Thing*, trans. Douglas V. Steere (1956; repr. n.p.: Rough Draft Publishing, 2013), 34.

Chapter 3: Sustain Your Parental Role

1. G. Klosinski, "Psychological Maltreatment in the Context of Separation and Divorce," *Child Abuse and Neglect* 17.4 (1993): 557–63.
2. Organization for Economic Co-operation and Development (OECD), "Families Are Changing," in OECD, ed., *Doing Better for Families* (Paris: OECD Publishing, 2011): 28.
3. A. Milevsky, M. Schlechter, S. Netter, and D. Keehn, "Maternal and Paternal Parenting Styles in Adolescents: Associations with Self-Esteem, Depression and Life-Satisfaction," *Journal of Child and Family Studies* 16.1 (2006): 39–47.
4. R. E. Larzelere, A. S. Morris, and A. W. Harrist, *Authoritative Parenting: Synthesizing Nurturance and Discipline for Optimal Child Development* (Washington, DC: American Psychological Association, 2012), 27.

Chapter 4: Provide Stability Through Nurturance

1. Hal Arkowitz and Scott O. Lilienfeld, "Is Divorce Bad for Children?" *Scientific American*, March 1, 2013, http://www.scientificamerican.com /article/is-divorce-bad-for-children/.
2. Sue Shellenbarger, "Not in Front of the Kids: Documenting the Emotional Toll of Parental Tension," *Wall Street Journal*, June 2005, http://www.wsj .com/articles/SB111947769017766924.

3. Paul R. Amato and Bruce Keith, "Parental Divorce and the Well-Being of Children: A Meta-Analysis," *Psychological Bulletin* 110.1 (1991): 26–46.

4. Janet R. Johnston, "Parental Alignments and Rejection: An Empirical Study of Alienation in Children of Divorce," *Journal of the American Academy of Psychiatry and the Law* 31.2 (2003): 158–170. Retrieved from http://www.jaapl.org/content/31/2/158.full.pdf+html.

Chapter 5: Regain Control—Reclaim Yourself

1. G. M. Gillespie, dir. and D. B. Rauber, ed., *A Judge's Guide: Making Child-Centered Decisions in Custody Cases* (Washington, DC: American Bar Association Center on Children and the Law, 2008), 16.

2. Mark Banschick, "The High Failure Rate of Second and Third Marriages," *Psychology Today*, February 6, 2012, https://www.psychologytoday.com /blog/the-intelligent-divorce/201202/the-high-failure-rate-second -and-third-marriages.

3. E. Mavis Hetherington and Anne Mitchell Elmore, "Risk and Resilience in Children Coping with Their Parents' Divorce and Remarriage" in ed. Sunia S. Luthar, *Resilience and Vulnerability Adaptation in the Context of Childhood Adversities* (Cambridge: Cambridge University Press, 2003), 182–212.

4. American Psychological Association, "Marriage and Divorce," APA.org, accessed March 27, 2015, http://www.apa.org/topics/divorce/.

5. Joan B. Kelly and Judith S. Wallerstein, "The Effects of Parental Divorce: Experiences of the Child in Early Latency," *American Journal of Orthopsychiatry* 46.1 (1976): 20–32.

Chapter 6: Realign Your Relationships

1. Richard A. Gardner, "Commentary on Kelly and Johnston's 'The Alienated Child: A Reformulation of Parental Alienation Syndrome,'" *Family Court Review* 42.4 (2004): 611–21.

Chapter 7: Redefine Parenting

1. Christopher L. Heffner, "Erikson's Stages of Psychosocial Development," AllPsych.com, accessed December 30, 2015, http://allpsych.com/ psychology101/social_development/.

2. Erik Erikson, *Childhood and Society* (New York: W. W. Norton and Co., 1963), 219.

3. David K. Carson and Mark T. Bittner, "Temperament and School-Aged Children's Coping Abilities and Responses to Stress," *Journal of Genetic Psychology* 155.3 (1994): 289–302.

4. Paul R. Amato, "Life-Span Adjustment of Children to Their Parents' Divorce," *Future of Children* 4.1 (1994): 143.

Chapter 8: Retain Your Parenthood in a Blended Family

1. Ron L. Deal, ed., "Marriage, Family, and Stepfamily Statistics," SmartStepfamilies.com, April 2014, http://www.smartstepfamilies.com /view/statistics.

2. E. Mavis Hetherington, "Coping with Marital Transitions: A Family Systems Perspective," *Monographs of the Society for Research in Child Development* 57.2–3 (1992): 1–14.

3. Cody C. Delistraty, "The Importance of Eating Together," *Atlantic*, July 18, 2014, http://www.theatlantic.com/health/archive/2014/07 /the-importance-of-eating-together/374256/.

4. Kelly Musick and Ann Meier, "Assessing Causality and Persistence in Associations Between Family Dinners and Adolescent Well-Being," *Journal of Marriage and Family* 74.3 (2012): 476–93.

Chapter 9: Preserve Loving Relationships

1. Judith S. Wallerstein, Julia M. Lewis, and Sandra Blakeslee, *The Unexpected Legacy of Divorce: The 25 Year Landmark Study* (New York: Hyperion, 2000).

2. Gary Chapman, *The Five Love Languages: How to Express Heartfelt Commitment to Your Mate* (Chicago: Northfield, 2004).

A Final Word

1. Doris Akers and Mahalia Jackson, "Lord, Don't Move the Mountain," 1958. Many variations of this piece exist, but to listen to a performance by Mahalia Jackson that closely resembles what Angelou sang, see "'Lord Don't Move The Mountain—Mahalia Jackson w/ choir," YouTube video, posted by "Rowoches," July 17, 2009, https://www.youtube.com /watch?v=a3AsPjDtmTQ.

ABOUT THE AUTHOR

JOHN CHIRBAN, THD, PHD, holds a doctorate with distinction from Harvard University in applied theology and another from Boston University's University Professors Program in clinical psychology and oral histories. The author of numerous research papers and professional articles, Dr. Chirban has written and edited more than a dozen books addressing human growth, relationships, and spirituality.

Teaching at Harvard University for more than twenty-five years about relationships, sexuality, and spirituality, he currently serves as part-time lecturer of psychology in the department of psychiatry at Harvard Medical School, director of Cambridge Counseling Associates, and professor emeritus of psychology at Hellenic College.

A guest on numerous radio and television programs, he appears frequently on *Dr. Phil* and *The Doctors* and has served on the advisory board for *Dr. Phil* since its inception.

A licensed clinical psychologist in California and Massachusetts, he is certified as a guardian ad litem in Massachusetts and lectures nationally before professional and lay audiences concerning relationships, sexuality, and spirituality.

His study of more than ten thousand children and parents has culminated in several ongoing publications on the impact of divorce on children.

Dr. Chirban lives with his three children, Alexis Georgia, Anthony Thomas, and Ariana Maria, in Carlisle, Massachusetts.